A PRACTICAL GUIDE TO BUILDING
A PROFITABLE ONLINE BUSINESS

# GETTING YOUR BUSINESS ON TRACK IN THE DIGITAL AGE

STERLYN MARKELL SMITH

ISBN: 978-1-7352942-2-3 (Paperback)
ISBN: 978-1-7352942-3-0 (eBook)

# DEDICATION

This book is dedicated to anyone looking to start a successful business online in a practical and step by step manner. Are you someone who is looking to fulfill your destiny by creating your own business? If you are that person and you're not sure how to begin, or you have run into some problems and challenges that are disrupting the process to your success, then this book is dedicated to you. This book can help you in many ways, including: **the business preparation process, mastering your finances, and understanding how money works.** Next, you will move on into the business empowerment tools that are needed to continue your success and gain momentum within your specific industry. Finally, you'll learn in a step-by-step manner how to successfully setup your internet business and make money with it. The last and final chapters of this book are about significant future trends that you need to understand and prepare for if you want to win in the E-commerce space and doing business in the digital age.

# ACKNOWLEDGMENTS

First, I would like to thank my God for creating me with a curious and analytical mindset, questioning and thinking deeply about everything presented to me in real-time to determine if it genuinely has real value. I want to thank my mother and father, who raised me to be the thoughtful and creative person that I've become today. I want to thank my son for motivating me to strive for more and to become the very best version of myself that I can be. I would also like to thank every friend and family member who has supported me throughout my life, especially those individuals who have prayed for me during the many challenging times. Thank you to everyone who believed in me, and believed in my ideas your support is greatly appreciated and well-received.

# INTRODUCTION

## Welcome to

## *Getting Your Business on Track in the Digital Age*

## A practical guide to building a profitable online business

Within the pages of this book, you will discover the help you need to become successful with your new online business. If you have ever wanted to learn how to become the best entrepreneur that you can be in the digital age, then you're reading the right book.

In full details, we will cover 3 of the essential business segments that you absolutely need to understand in order to succeed in business today and into the future. We will be covering the following valuable and important segments.

- **Financial mastery and the preparation process**
- **The business empowerment tools that will help you to succeed**
- **Business success and the growing trends of the future**

At the end of this reading *Getting Your Business on Track in the Digital Age*, you will have a clear understanding about how to overcome financial hurdles and business challenges that hold so many people back from living their dreams. You will learn some very valuable information regarding how to manage and control your debts, spending habits, and come up with a plan for investing into your businesses future. You will also learn how to think exactly like the rich do, which is why they remain wealthy, and the rest of society struggles to make ends meet.

We will also cover many of the future trends you need to be aware of in the world of E-commerce and online shopping that can make or break your business. You will learn the many different success habits of wealthy people that you can easily apply to your own life that will open your mind and elevate your thinking to a higher level. We also cover many other valuable subjects for your personal and business success, like email marketing and future trends you need to know and how to get started with them very quickly.

Get ready for a wealth of knowledge and financial trends that will help you succeed and take your business to the next level. Welcome to *Getting Your Business on Track in the Digital Age*.

## Our personal journey through life and in business

We will all be presented with various tests and challenges in life and business that we must face, which might be very tough to overcome. There may be times when these challenges can distract you from your path to accomplishing your goals and completing your dreams. If this happens, you must get back on track and persevere through them. You don't want to allow any problems or challenges to hold you back from your path to success that you have set out for yourself in your business and personal life.

Within the pages of this book, you will find detailed answers for helping you to prepare for success within your own business and some very important information for dealing with the various challenges that many of us must face in the world of business.

- Learn how to prepare yourself for the coming economic collapse that may be coming sooner than you think and right around the corner.
- Learn about the entrepreneur's mindset and the eight pillars to success.
- Learn about negotiation skills that can close deals for you.
- Learn how to make money and become successful with affiliate marketing.
- Learn how to overcome the challenges within your business after COVID 19.
- You will also learn the power of landing pages and how they convert to sales.
- Learn everything you need to know about E-commerce and the future of online shopping.
- Learn about the secrets of money and how it really works.
- Learn how to take ownership over your credit score and get your numbers up.
- You will also learn about the power of closing the sale.
- You will learn some new ideas regarding the ten millionaire success habits that are absolutely invaluable.
- Learn the difference between people with creative minds versus the educated mind.
- Learn how to get your customers to keep buying from you forever.

*Getting your business on track in the digital age* is a self-help book that covers many business topics that are very easy to digest. You will see how we bring together the best business tools that are available, and you will learn how to overcome various business issues that can help anyone turn their challenges around and use them to win and succeed. Many of the subjects we're covering in this book will empower you within your business operations, and you'll learn how to take actionable steps that have been holding individuals back from gaining the success that they have always wanted.

The information provided within this book is timely, practical and very useful and you'll see that the resources we've provided you with at the end of this book are entirely relevant for those individuals who are looking for business, educational and financial resources that will help them to achieve their goals. Upon completing this book, you should start living a more empowered business life for sure. Don't wait another minute! Start today and begin taking ownership and control over your business journey. Welcome to *Getting Your Business on Track in the Digital Age.*

# CONTENTS

# SECTION 2: THE BUSINESS EMPOWERMENT TOOLS TO SUCCESS

# SECTION 3: BUSINESS SUCCESS IN THE DIGITAL ECONOMY & THE GROWING TRENDS

# SECTION 1

## FINANCIAL MASTERY & THE PREPARATION PROCESS

# CHAPTER 1

# LEARN THE 7 FINANCIAL SKILLS YOU SHOULD HAVE BEEN TAUGHT IN HIGH SCHOOL
## (THAT THEY DIDN'T TEACH YOU)

The United States public school system is the place where most of us should have been adequately educated and trained in the very important fields of business start-up, business sustainability, personal finance skills, and investment knowledge. We should have learned how to save and budget our money and manage our personal finances. These are very essential skills in our lives that we use daily which so many Americans remain ignorant about because they don't understand financial intelligence. Learning these valuable subjects would have helped so many working-class Americans who struggle with debt and their bills every month. The U.S. Board of Education should have made these valuable subjects a top priority within our school curriculum while we were in high school. Unfortunately, most of us have never learned these valuable subjects proficiently, and the lack of this important financial knowledge keeps so many Americans broke and struggling financially every year.

Did you know that 67% of American families don't even have $1,000 available to them in their bank accounts just in case an actual emergency were to happen to them today?

Did you also know that many Americans are paying vast sums of their income on expensive mortgages, student loans, credit card payments, and auto loans? This is not a great position you want to be in if you're going to become financially independent and for building up your own personal wealth.

We will now look at the seven fundamental financial skills that most of us should have studied in high school, but never did because the U.S. public school system never taught us these essential financial skills. However, they have heavily pushed basic ideas like their common core, which is currently being emphasized in schools all across the country today. It's far more important that everyday working-class people learn how to manage their finances, learn about the various investment opportunities, and have some valuable business skills rather than learning unproductive common core skills. Unfortunately, most American's who went through the public school system never had the chance to master these important financial skills or subjects. They remain ignorant even today about how money and finances really work.

## The seven financial skills you should have learned in high school?

1.  **The importance of credit cards and interest rates-** Millions of American's are currently struggling to make their monthly bill payments and payments on their credit cards every month. According to the Federal Reserve Bank, millions of Americans owe more than 1.04 trillion dollars in credit card debt as of March 2019. On average, the typical American owes about $7,000 Dollars on bank credit cards alone. The problem arises when there is no self-control within these individuals, and most people just swipe their credit

cards and go. They don't realize that they are racking up a ton of interest payments on each of these credit cards that they swipe so easily. People who generally make charges on these credit cards are usually making the minimum monthly payments. Whenever you're only making the minimum payment each month, it will take you forever to pay them off with all the monthly reoccurring interest rate charges. Be very careful with your credit cards as they will keep you in debt and the poor house.

2. **Building up your credit score-** Your credit fico score is your financial report card for how well you manage your money and pay your bills on time. The fico score, on average, ranges between (300-850). A good fico score is (700) and above, with this type of high score it shows lending institutions that they can be confident that you will repay your future debts as promised. A (300-579) is a very poor score, and lending institutions may give you a hard time when it comes to getting a loan with this low score. A (580-669) is a fair rating, making it a little easier to qualify for loans with a basic interest rate. A (670-739) is a good rating, and lending institutions will gladly give you a loan with a good interest rate and flexible payment options. A (800-850) is an excellent rating for the fico score, and lending institutions will roll out the red carpet for anyone with this type of excellent rating. Learn all you can about your credit score and the many different ways that you can try to get your numbers up into the 800-fico score rating.

3. **Learning how to budget properly-** Budgeting is critical to anyone's financial success. The basic of budgeting is to understand exactly where your money is coming from, including your (income), and clearly understanding where it's going your (expenses). If you learn how to develop a reasonable budget to live within, it will help you to monitor your spending habits more closely. By doing this you may be able to cut back and conserve money within your

finances. Remember, don't spend money on things that you don't need. Developing a good budget will act as your personal regulator when dealing with your wealth and personal finances.

4. **Learning how to balance your checkbook-** Balancing your checkbook is very simple. You must understand every detail regarding your bank account and know how much money you have in it at all times. As money is coming into your account and going out from it, you must track how much is available daily. You never want to overdraft your account and start to bounce checks because you're not tracking the incoming and outgoing transactions. Bouncing a check is not good for you or your bank account. Bouncing checks can even negatively affect your credit score if you're not very careful. Balancing your checkbook is a very important thing to learn and understand, so you never get into financial trouble in the future.

5. **The basic of the compound interest- The rule of (72)** is a powerful financial concept to understand that will increase your finances exponentially over time. If, for example, you invest $10,000 dollars of your income at a 10% rate of return annually into an investment vehicle that has compounded interest that money will grow over time and in (7) years, your money will double in value to $20,000 dollars. Compound interest is a modern-day miracle that can make anyone wealthy that is invested in the right investment vehicle. Compound interest will make anyone wealthy with a little patience, perseverance, and over a specific time at the right compound interest rate. While in high school, if most of us understood compound interest, we could have started saving and investing our money while we were young, which could have changed our financial future dramatically. How unfortunate we didn't learn this important information while we were in grade or high school.

6. **Investing our money-** Most millionaires and billionaires are heavily invested into stocks and bonds, mutual funds, and ETF's. Paper assets are the number one asset class that wealthy people invest into Outside of purchasing and investing in very large real estate projects. One of the top asset classes that the wealthy are heavily invested into is hard assets like: gold, platinum, and silver, which hold their value year after year. Some individuals have become very wealthy and well off from investing their money into these various asset classes. Learning how to choose a good investment, and allowing it to maximize and grow over time would have been an amazing thing to have learned in high school for so many struggling Americans.

7. **Starting a Business-** The entire world operates and runs on businesses and corporations that offer their products and services to their willing and able customers. Everyone of us who has a job works for a company or a corporation established by someone or a group of people who had an idea. While we were in high school, why weren't we taught about business start-up, business finance, and business marketing? If we understood basic business budgeting, customer service skills, and basic marketing skills, this could have been very helpful for so many of us. We could have started our businesses instead of working for someone else. Only if the school curriculum and our teachers properly educated us regarding these important concepts. At the same time, while we were young, many of us could have been much further along in our lives with the knowledge about how to start a successful business.

In closing, the high schools within the U.S. are teaching their students basic subjects that may be easily forgotten if they are not experienced and practiced regularly. Not many of the public schools are making sure their students are learning these important financial subjects that we've just discussed in this chapter. These valuable and important subjects could have enhanced the students' lives if they had this very valuable information. While in school, most of us should have learned how to manage and increase our finances. At this time, the only thing any of us can do is take it upon ourselves and learn these important subjects on our own. Once we understand how money really works, we can begin to take complete ownership of our financial future.

Do you want to change your financial IQ and understand how money really works? You should take a look at our empowerment resources at the end of this book to discover some very powerful resources that can aid you in your financial growth. We have included some of the best finance and business start-up books and other resources out there for the beginner and the seasoned financial veteran. We have created this resource list for those individuals who want to take back control over their finances and life in general. We are sure you will not be disappointed with the resources that we've carefully researched for you.

# CHAPTER 2

# MONEY SECRETS
## LEARN HOW MONEY REALLY WORKS

The dictionary definition of money is- A currency and medium of exchange in the form of coins and banknotes.

Most of us work very hard every day on our jobs and within our businesses trying to earn and increase our prosperity, wealth, and financial resources. What is money? For most of us, money is simply a tool used to exchange goods and services that we need to survive and live on. 90% of working-class Americans and millions of people worldwide get up every day and go to work on their jobs to earn money that maintains and sustains their lifestyles. We follow this routine by working on a job for someone else to make a living for our survival. We earn money in exchange for our time, energy, and our skill-sets.

The desire for money is the driving force behind so many things we do as human beings and for many of the things we need. Everyone's drive and desire to make money is what keeps the world operating the way it does. This happens through purchasing goods and services that we all need to pay for to survive, such as: **shelter, food, clothing, transportation, and entertainment.**

## Understanding how the rich stay wealthy

Many of the rich people within our society remain wealthy because they have had the opportunity to spend more of their time developing new ways to generate increased revenue streams that bring in more money and financial opportunities that keep them wealth. The working poor within our society generally remain in their condition because they don't have the time, proper training, education, and understanding about how money works and how to increase their finances through the various new business ventures, ideas, and investment opportunities that may be available to them. Many working-class individuals don't spend enough of their time trying to develop their skill-sets and learning about financial knowledge that will increase their wealth. You must spend some time brain-storming over ideas that you can bring to the market place, which can increase your finances. The rich are heavily invested into revenue-generating opportunities that can increase and expand for them over time.

## Understanding the rules of money

There is a rule to money that the wealthy understand very well. The rule is that money comes to those who understand how it works and to those individuals who know how to make money work for them instead of them working for it. The secret to getting money to move into your direction is to first, learn as much as you can about how to keep more of the money you already earn through your employer based on your personal income. Secondly, you must learn how to maximize and in-crease your finances through financial assets that payout consistently. You must develop knowledge about future investment opportunities that can increase your wealth in value over time through the power of compound interest.

## Following the path of the wealthy

Many wealthy people who have money and financial resources readily available to them spend very little of their time worrying like the rest of us about the rising cost of living, financial debts, and the monthly bills that we owe on. The wealthy don't have these problems because they have a complete understanding about the important rules of money. They are invested heavily into asset classes that increase in value over time. This knowledge leaves them with more than enough money working in their favor, so they don't have to work hard for money. Many of them focus more of their time and energy on growing their wealth by getting high returns from their increasing assets. One of the most popular ways the wealthy protect their money and their financial assets is through setting up a living trust. A living trust is a financial instrument that you set up with a professional, which allows you to protect your money exclusively. The living trust is one secure way that the rich can hide their wealth from the public's eyes that may be looking to see what they own. It also protects their wealth from thieves who want to rob them, and it even protects their money from lawsuits they may be involved in at some time in their lives.

## The lack of wealth problem that so many people have

When you think back to when you were younger in your high school years, how much time was spent in your classrooms or at home with your parents learning about how money works. Most of us learned very little regarding financial asset classes, savings accounts, and investment opportunities.

For most of us, little time was spent learning about these valuable subjects or gaining a basic understanding about how money works and how to increase our assets. When we were in school, we mainly learned about basic arithmetic, English classes, and core science classes. Many of us had minimal time and training spent learning about the value of a savings account, budgeting our money, and investing for the future. Since so many Americans had no financial education as a youth, this is the primary explanation why many struggle with saving money and money management today. They never had the proper training, understanding, and information they needed regarding how money works and how to make it work in their favor.

## Understanding how the system was setup

If you're paying close attention, you might be aware that we live in a society where government officials, financial institutions, big bankers, and very large corporations secretly make many of the rules that we follow and live under. If you were born in America, you understand how the richest families who were here before established the American business structure, the government systems, the financial system, and the media industries that we see every day. Most of us didn't learn about the structure of these systems and how they really worked while we were in school and most of us didn't develop much financial education while living at home with our parents, who only had basic jobs themselves. We were not told about the advantages of managing our own money and starting a profitable company. Because of this lack of knowledge, we just learned how to become employees and consumers and search for work to support our lives just as our parents did.

## Money is required for everything that you use in society

We all understand that any material possession that we actually own was purchased with money that we have earned or someone else has received by working on a job or by someone who has a company that they own for the average middle-class American. Many Americans go to public schools that aren't getting the kind of valuable education they need to be independent of a job. Learning about money and finances should have been one of the most important subjects that we all should have been taught while in high school since everything we need and use requires money. This is very important since our entire lives and daily survival revolve around money that we must earn and the material goods you can and cannot afford to purchase unless you have the financial resources available to you. Let's look at a small list of those things that require our money.

- Money is required to eat and feed you and your family because all food products come at a cost.
- Money is required for shelter and housing to live wherever you currently reside.
- Money is required to purchase healthcare and medicine if you ever get sick.
- Money is required for vehicles and transportation to get you from one place to another.
- Money is required to pay for government taxes, city roads and highways, public schools, and senior retirement benefits such as social security and Medicare.
- Money is required if you decide to have a family and want to raise children someday.
- •Money is required to purchase clothing, shoes, household goods, vacations, and entertainment whenever you need them.
- Money is also required even upon your death; it cost to die as well.

You can now understand why learning about money and financial prosperity is so important within our society since there is nothing we can do without it in our lives.

## Learning the language of money

We should all learn the language of money as quickly as we can. If you want to begin the process of increasing your financial knowledge, you must learn to speak the language of money by understanding some very important financial terms and concepts.

**Best sites to learn about money**

https://www.investopedia.com
https://www.thebalance.com
https://www.thoughtco.com/economics-4133521
https://www.cengage.com
https://www.moneycrashers.com
https://www.mymoney.gov/Pages/default.aspx
https://www.khanacademy.org
https://www.ally.com
https://www.betterment.com

- **Accounting-** A comprehensive recording of financial transactions about a business.
- **Return on investment-** A ratio between net profits and the cost of an investment.
- **Depreciation-** A reduction in the value of an asset over time.
- **Cost of goods sold-** Refers to the direct cost of the production of goods sold in a company.
- **Retained earnings-** The Amount of net income left over for the business after paying out dividends to shareholders.
- **Accounts payable-** Money owed by a company to its creditors.
- **Accounts Receivable-** Money owed to a company by its debtors.
- **Compound interest-** Interest paid on the interest is the result of reinvesting interest.

You must understand the language of money if you want to be in control of your financial future. Learn all that you can about money so you can master it and not have it mastering you.

## The expansion of your money and financial knowledge

If you want your money and finances to increase, you cannot take what you earn and lock it into a safe and think that it will generate wealth for you. You must learn how to increase your money through your business and increasing investment assets.

- **Business-** To expand your money in the world of business, you can take what you've earned and reinvest it back into your own company to grow your business, which can increase your revenue and wealth potential. The other thing you can do is invest into another successful business idea that has good earning potential and develop it into a company that can generate revenue for you.

  Take a look at these great sites to help you start your own business

  https://www.business.com
  https://www.allbusiness.com
  https://www.legalzoom.com
  https://www.franchisegator.com
  https://www.liveplan.com
  https://www.rocketlawyer.com
  https://www.incfile.com
  https://www.corpnet.com
  https://www.mycorporation.com
  https://www.g2.com

- **Investments-** There are many different types of unique investment options to choose from in the market place. You will need to discover the right one that fits your investment goals and one that will help you to manage the right amount of risk that you're comfortable with based on the capital you want to invest. Listed below are some of the very popular investment companies to take a look at.

### Great investment websites

https://us.etrade.com/home
https://www.stash.com/
https://robinhood.com/us/en/
https://www.m1finance.com/
https://www.schwab.com/
https://www.axosinvest.com/
https://fundrise.com/

1. Stocks and Bonds
2. ETF's and bank certificates of deposit (CD)
3. Real estate investments and property rentals
4. Hard assets like gold, silver, and platinum
5. Digital and crypto currencies

## Learning from the Money Gurus

There are many people who are not very comfortable taking control over and managing their own personal finances. If you're someone who isn't very comfortable making financial decisions that can affect your money and its growth, be aware there are many qualified professional individuals and finance companies out on the market that are paid a small commission fee to help you maximize and increase your financial assets.

- CPA- Certified Public Accountant- https://www.aicpa.org
- CFP- Certified Financial Planner - https://nasba.org
- Stock Market Broker - http://www.nastockbrokers.com/
- Hedge Fund Managers - http://www.nastockbrokers.com/
- Wealth Managers - https://www.napfa.org/
- Robo-Advisors- https://www.consumersadvocate.org/robo-advisors

Try to invest some valuable time into finding the right financial advisor to help you achieve your own financial goals based on the level of risk that works for you. Contact and consult with them until you're sure you have found the one that understands your exact personal investment strategy. Also, read all the books that you can about money and investing. They are worth their weight in gold.

## Amazon's best finance books of all time.

https://www.amazon.com/s?k=best+finance+books+of+all+-time&crid=LWBX7BTX05KR&sprefix=best+finance+books%-2Caps%2C204&ref=nb_sb_ss_ts-a-p_3_18

# CHAPTER 3

# THE MONEY DECEPTION
## BELIEVING THE PERCEPTION THAT MONEY HAS REAL VALUE

The almighty dollar, everyone is working harder and harder on their jobs and within their businesses, because we all want more money to increase our wealth and income potential.

In America and many other countries worldwide, people are working long and hard hours on their jobs and within their businesses trying to earn all the money or fiat currency that they can to sustain and maintain their lifestyles. We are all working very hard for the money because everything we need and desire for our survival requires money and finances to get it.

- **Did you know that the U.S. dollar isn't backed by anything other than debt? Every bank-created dollar within our bank accounts is the result of an open loan. When a bank creates a loan, they simply mark up a borrower's account (a bank liability) and hold the borrower's promissory note on their asset side. Our dollars are not backed up by gold, oil, real estate, or food commodities with real asset value. Since 1971, our dollars are no longer backed by anything other than the belief that it has real value and nothing else.**

The value of money is an illusion that is not backed up by real tangibles or valuable assets like gold and silver, crude oil, food commodities or real estate, and land values. The Federal Reserve is a private corporate entity that's not owned by our government or our politicians.

**The Federal Reserve System is not "owned" by anyone. The Federal Reserve was created in 1913 by the Federal Reserve Act to serve as the nation's central bank. The Board of Governors in Washington, D.C., is an agency of the federal government and reports to and is directly accountable to the Congress.** Their sole responsibility is to print and produce the money that we all use here in the United States to pay for our goods and services that we use every day. The Federal Reserve is also the entity responsible for setting the countries interest rates, which dictates how much we get charged by the banks when we need to take out expensive loans for things such as cars and homes. If you want to fully understand The Federal Reserve's history and when and how it was established, check out the link below. You will also learn about the petrodollar and when the U.S. came off of the gold standard. Read these important and historical articles from the sites we have listed below.

- https://www.federalreserveeducation.org/about-the-fed/history
- https://www.thebalance.com/what-is-a-petrodollar-3306358
- https://www.history.com/this-day-in-history/fdr-takes-united-statesoff-gold-standard

Within this brief chapter, we're going to cover an overview and give you a basic understanding about the deception of money, and how many of us have been fooled into believing it has real value.

## Chasing the almighty dollar

Most America's who have working-class parents who went to public school were not taught about how things really work within our society. Our school teachers work for and are the employees of the government agency called the U.S. Department of Education. We were taught by these educators and teachers what it means to survive and make money in this country. The basics were to get good grades while you're in school, then someday you can go to college graduate and get a good-paying job to take care of yourself and your family if you happen to have one. Most working-class Americans have been taught this information from teachers and our government officials. Many of us believe that working for someone else and just getting a job is the only way to survive and earn a living today. Many of us didn't learn about business start-up, increasing our finances through assets, and investing our money for the future, which could have been a game-changer while we were in school. Many Americans are still stuck, believing that they must depend on someone else or the government to make it in this life because of what they were taught.

- **Did anyone ever teach you that there is another way to get your money to work for you? Did you know that you can become wealthy through investments and the power of compounded interest over time?**
- **Did you know that some investment options will pay you monthly dividends that you can live on for the rest of your life if that investment remains solid and increases in value?**
- **When you were in high school, did you ever learn anything about business, finance, and investing from your teachers?**
- **Did they teach you anything in your math classes about how money works and how to get it to work for you?**
- **When you were in high school, were you taught anything about how to invest the money you've earned from your job to increase your wealth?**

Most of us were never taught anything about how money works. The one thing we were all taught for sure is how to be good hardworking employees and how to get a job working for someone else to earn a living. The other thing most of us were taught in school is how to make an impression on our bosses so we can hopefully get a larger paycheck, a bonus, or a raise while playing the good employee role.

## The more you make, the more you spend

Since they weren't taught how money really works, many Americans, whenever they get a raise or a bonus or even a promotion, the first thing most of them choose to do is spend it all rather than saving it or investing it to increase their wealth for the future. So many Americans will immediately go out to buy a new car, a new home, or even the latest electronic gadget that hits the market instead of saving their increases for the future.

Many Americans don't realize that the wealthy families and those at the top of the food chain have somewhat rigged the game in their favor. They keep you the consumer spending every dime you make right back into their companies and corporations that keep you broke and struggling to make ends meet every month. Don't get trapped in the rat race that the elites have setup for you. Don't spend all of your hard-earned cash in their stores, making them richer while you continue to get poorer every day. Learn all that you can about how money works and how you can save and invest what you make to increase your wealth.

## How an economic crash can kill
## the value of your dollars

Since the economic crash of 2008/2009 happened, have you noticed how many other economic fluctuations and financial hits the stock market has had since that time?

- https://www.ft.com/global-economy
- https://www.usnews.com/news/economy

Did you know there has been more than ten big Dow Jones financial hits since 2008, and there are more to come within the turbulent economic times we're currently living in? There is presently the rising cost of living going up about 3% annually. The value of our dollars continue to decrease over time. We must all take it upon ourselves to learn how to protect ourselves and conserve our wealth as best we can.

## The steps to finding balance

The American dollar or the fiat currency is at the core of the financial system that we use in the United States. The various governments worldwide are responsible for printing the money that's needed to run their own countries and keep their economies operating efficiently. Sometimes these foreign and domestic government officials don't manage their economies very well, creating a financial crash or financial collapse. When this happens, hyper-inflation and even a depression can affect the economy of that country.

Here are some things you can do to find balance within your financial portfolio, no matter what the state of the economy is within your country.

1. **Save more money than you spend with every paycheck that you earn.**
2. **Invest into hard assets like gold, silver, and other precious metals when you can.**
3. **Purchase some investment real estate and rent it out for a profit and some residual income.**
4. **If you have an extra room within your home, you could consider renting out a room.**
5. **Create an emergency fund just in case something unfortunate happens, you want to be prepared.**
6. **You can purchase or start an online business that has future growth potential. You just need to do some careful research.**

In closing, try to take complete ownership over your personal and business finances and try not to depend on the government or your job for your financial security. Remember, money is an illusion that's not backed by anything tangible like gold or silver, oil, basic food commodities, or even real estate values. If the system ever collapses on itself, you don't want to be caught off guard, so be prepared.

# CHAPTER 4

# HOW TO START A BUSINESS WITH NO MONEY

**Starting a business with no money down, is that even possible?**

**The answer to this question is- Yes!**

## There are three ways to start a real business with no money down, which are the following:

1. You inherit a business from a family member or a friend that is already running, operational, and making money with its own products or services and customer base.

2. You have been offered or gifted a business by someone who would like to retire or step into a new direction in their lives.

3. Your skills pay you enough money to invest into your own start-up business. In this capacity of starting your own business, you could be someone who has a special skill-set that gets you paid because your skills are in high demand. An example would be a software developer who creates programs on the side and after work hours when people need your services. Another example would be an auto

mechanic who works on cars at his job, and when he is off work offers his services to individuals on the weekends and after hours to earn the extra money to start his business.

These are the three main ways to start a business with no extra money on hand. If option (3) is the way you want go, you may have to put in some extra hours and hard work on your days off from your day job to meet your goals, but it is possible.

In this chapter, we will look at the easiest ways to start a business with little to no liquid capital necessary to get started. Don't be fooled. There is always an initial cost to start up, operate, and maintain any business large or small.

## The seven core ways to generate the money to start your business

Starting a business can be done in ways that don't have to break your wallet or bank account. Whatever type of business you're trying to start-up, you don't want it to cause you to go into debt to get it launched and off the ground. We will now look at the seven core ways to get your business up and running with little to no cost to you, the entrepreneur. Let's get into it.

1. **Borrowing money from your 401-K:** If you work for a company and have a job at this time, most of them offer a (401k) plan where you can save money towards retirement. Many people don't realize that with most (401k) plans, you can take out loans from within them to help you pay for important things you may need to take care of before you retire. Talk to your (401k) administrator to see what the qualifications are for you to take out a loan to start your own business. You will have to pay back this loan, of course, but you'll be paying back yourself these loan payments with interest until it's fully paid back. This is one of the best ways to pay for any high-ticket items you need to purchase or even use it for something

like starting a business. Take some time to investigate your (401k) as a viable option for starting your own business.

2. **Get a second Job:** One of the fastest ways to earn the money you need to start your own business is by getting a second job. There are various options available to you in today's economy other than just punching a clock and having a second boss to report to. You can drive your car for Uber or Lyft services if needed. You can make package deliveries by joining up with Amazon and supporting their delivery services. You can deliver food with Grub Hub and other vendors that offer these types of services, and there are so many more to choose from. Take some time to assess what options there are out there for you to take advantage of.

https://www.uber.com
https://www.lyft.com
https://flex.amazon.com
https://driver.grubhub.com

3. **Crowd funding:** If you don't know about it already, let me introduce you to crowd funding the practice of funding a project or a business venture by raising small amounts of money from various people worldwide. The people who believe in your ideas are typically done on the Internet through a crowd funding platform. This is a great way to get the money you need to start your business if you have no funding, to begin with, and you have a great idea that you believe in that you want to bring to the market. All you need to do is take your ideas and marketing plans and put this information on the crowd funding platform available to you. People worldwide can go to the crowd funding platform and see your ideas and donate to you or your business at a small cost to you for using the platform.

https://www.blackbaud.com
https://www.kickstarter.com
https://www.indiegogo.com
https://www.gofundme.com
https://www.crowdsupply.com
https://www.crowdfunder.com
https://experiment.com
https://www.chuffed.org/us
https://www.customink.com -Fundraising Ideas
https://www.supportful.com

4. **Yard sale/garage sale:** You can make money from your old stuff that you have in your storage or things that you've collected over the years that you really don't need any longer. There is a saying that goes: **"One man's trash is, another man's treasure."** We all have things we have hidden in our closets, storage lockers, and our backyards that we're hanging on to that we honestly will never use. Why not sell these things to someone else that can use them and take the cash you get from the sale to setup and launch that business that you have always said you were going to start? Now you can do it with the money you make from selling all the old items you may have collected over the years.

5. **Raising capital with investors:** If you have a great idea and a solid business plan, why not present your idea to a venture capital firm or a philanthropist who could fund your business overnight. Suppose they believe in you and your vision the same way that you do. Usually, when going this route, individuals or companies are generally looking for ideas that can generate a high Return on Investment (ROI). They are looking for something that can help them increase their profit potential.

https://lp.lendio.com
https://www.inventmyidea.com

https://www.equitynet.com
https://www.funded.com
https://angel.co
https://www.seedinvest.com
https://www.startengine.com
https://circleup.com
https://wefunder.com

6. **Borrowing from Family members:** This is one of the oldest ways in history for people to get the capital they need who want to start a business. Borrowing from family members can be risky and cause problems with relationships if the business fails, and all the money invested gets lost. You want to be very careful putting yourself and your family members in a tough financial situation if you honestly don't believe in your ideas or have a backup plan for your business if it fails to deliver as promised. This can be a great thing working in your favor with your family members if the business is successful because now you both can feel excited about the fact that the business is a win.

7. **Small Business Administration (SBA) https://www.sba.gov:** The SBA is a government organization that will give funding to those individuals who want to start their own businesses in 5 different ways below. You'll need to be very serious about your business and your ideas, and you must have an excellent business plan to get any money from the government. They will often require that you have at least 25%-30% of the start-up capital needed to run the business.

- **Loans-** Start or expand your business with loans guaranteed by the Small Business Administration. Use Lender Match to find lenders that offer loans for your business.
- **Investment Capital-** Find an investor for your business through a Small Business Investment Company (SBIC) licensed by the Small Business Administration (SBA).

- **Disaster Assistance-** The SBA provides low-interest disaster loans to help businesses and homeowners recover from declared disasters.
- **Surety Bonds-** The Small Business Administration (SBA) guarantees bid, performance, and payment surety bonds issued by certain surety companies.
- **Grants-** The SBA works with different organizations to provide grants for small businesses. Find out if you meet the requirements to apply.

In closing, if you want to start a business, the first thing you must do is create an excellent business plan with all the details about how you're going to start-up, run and manage your business. Next, you want to secure the proper funding for your business, whether it's from working a second job, getting some investors to fund you, or even borrowing from your family members. Whatever decision you make, remember there are no short cuts to success in life. It takes (3) things to be successful at it and that is hard work, a business plan and the action steps to get things done. Don't wait! Get started today to make your dream business come to life.

# CHAPTER 5

# HOW TO KEEP YOUR BUSINESS UP AND OPERATIONAL AND WHAT TO DO IF IT FAILS?

T here is an awesome and amazing feeling when starting your own business, but it can also be a very scary time when you realize that you're on your own and in business for yourself.

Becoming a business owner can be one of the greatest feelings or maybe even the scariest moments in your life when you realize that you're your own boss now, and you will be in complete control over your destiny and financial future. Many business owners desire to be in this position because, now they don't have to answer to someone else any longer because they are the boss and in the driver's seat now. Before you get too excited, let's look at some very important statistics you need to understand regarding starting your own business. Did you know that about 20 percent of all small businesses fail within their first year of operation? Did you also know that by the end of the fifth year, about 50 percent of small businesses go under as well? According to the SBA- Small Business Administration records, there are about 30 plus million small businesses in the U.S. today. That number at times increases or decreases depending on the up or down movement of the U.S. economy.

The question is, why do these businesses fail, and what is the reason for them closing their doors? The truth is there can be numerous financial and business reasons that these business owners have to close their doors. We will look at some of them now.

**Here are some of the top reasons why so many small businesses fail in the first five years.**

- **Lack of financial capital and running out of money is a huge reason.**
- **No one is buying their products and or services any longer.**
- **The business is overextended- they have too much overhead and expenses.**
- **The business, if faced with legal issues or pending lawsuits can break or dismantle the company and cause a bankruptcy.**
- **The business plan didn't account for the competition, there is no relevancy for the products and services that they are selling, or the marketing strategy is dead, and no one is buying.**

There can be numerous other reasons that a business has to close its doors. There are too many to list here. One of the less critical reasons for a business closure is when the owner is up in age or very elderly, and they can't keep up with the day to day business operations any longer. They may want to retire, but don't have any kids or relatives to leave the business to so they just close the doors and call it quits.

## How to make sure your business will not fail

Some of the most important rules to consider when starting a business are to evaluate and assess the probability that the business can succeed within the current economic climate. You will have to answer some very important questions like the following.

- How good and relevant are your products or services? Do they meet the needs of your customers?
- What do you know about your competitors, and how many of them are there in the market? What are you doing differently than they are? What makes your product or service stand out better than the competition?
- What about your technology is your business operating with the latest and best technology applications to succeed in your market? Do you have a contingency plan if something better comes along and challenges your business model?
- What about the economy if it tanks what plans do you have to remain relevant? Do you have a backup financial plan for your current financing if things go south?

These are just a few of the things you should consider if you decide to start a business and want it to work out in your favor, and you want to be successful.

If you want to succeed in business, you should be able to answer these questions at the least and have a contingency plan for the following important items; these can greatly impact your businesses success.

- Not creating a backup plan for running out of sustainable cash flow?
- Businesses that have the wrong management team in place?
- Allowing your business to get out priced by the competition or the market that you serve?
- Businesses that are not satisfying unhappy customers with their products or services?
- Having a bad marketing strategy and not getting more customers to expand your business?
- No future plans for business expansion and production growth?
- No backup financing or liquid capital for emergencies that may happen?

- **Not enough cash flow for overcoming legal hurdles and business challenges?**

## Understanding your business plan and its importance

**The power of your business plan-** Putting your business plan in place and considering the list of items we have just discussed might be something for you to consider in the future of planning and running your business. Success could be within your grasp if you actually follow your plan.

**Keep your expenses as low as possible-** Don't over extend yourself financially. You must monitor your daily and monthly operating cost for the success of your business. You may need to cut back in some areas where you can conserve some cash flow.

**Remember that your customers are number one-** Always remember that you are in business because of your customers. They are the individuals that are spending their hard-earned dollars buying your products and services, so make them and their issues the top priority within your business at all times.

**You must expand and increase your sales regularly-** You must remember that you are in business to make money and create a sustainable business for you and your family. You want to try very hard to find new ways to expand and grow your sales, product lines, and your business services as often as you can. By doing this, you can increase your business revenue and keep it moving in an upward and positive direction.

In closing, starting a business isn't very easy, but with the right business plan in place and the right team of management and leaders, you can be successful. Just as important as a business plan and your leadership team is to your success, you also need an excellent line of products and services that you offer to your customer base. If you do everything correctly, your chances of success can increase exponentially. Start today! You must begin the planning process for your business and its success, and you just might make a ton of money and become very successful.

# CHAPTER 6

# HOW IS YOUR ECONOMY
## ARE YOU PROPERLY PROTECTED?

**M**ost people are very aware that we are living in uncertain financial times right now in America and in many countries worldwide. Let's take a look at a shortlist of the issues going on right now that can affect your finances and your personal economy.

- The U.S. government deficit is currently at 27 Trillion and rising daily.
- There is the current threat of war with other countries like China, Russia, and Iran.
- There is a rise in unemployment, layoffs, poverty, and the increase in crime rates that are affecting many cities in America and other countries worldwide.
- There is a constant threat of government shutdowns and trade wars with other countries like China and Mexico.
- Fluctuations in the stock market and the constantly increasing interest rates.
- Inflation rising at about 3% annually and the rising cost of food and living expenses.
- The increases in state sales taxes and government taxes fluctuating regularly.

These are just a few of the current known factors that can have a major effect on everyone's finances and their economic situation, whether they like it or not.

## What the economist has to say

Nearly every economist and investment banker around the world are all saying the same thing right now. They say that there is a huge financial crash or meltdown right around the corner that will dramatically affect the global economy when it does.

The main cause of this crash will be based on some known factors, such as the huge financial deficits that so many governments operate within around the world. Then, there is the quantitative easing that these governments have pushed into the financial markets, driving up inflation and causing instability in many of the different stock markets around the world.

Many economists say that the next financial crash will be much bigger than the one we all experienced in the 2008/2009 subprime housing and financial crisis twelve years ago. That crisis alone practically destroyed many of the middle-class families and homeowners within our society. The last major crisis created many more impoverished people who need government assistance and government aid to survive and make it each month.

## The Rise in Technology and Artificial Intelligence (AI)

The other major concern that many people should be aware of today is the rise of new WIFI technologies like (5G) and the increasing dependence on Artificial Intelligence (Robots) within our society. These changes will affect us all and eliminate huge sectors of jobs currently being held by humans right now. The studies show that by 2030, there will be about 20%- 25% of the current jobs held by humans that will be lost to robots and robotic technologies within the next ten years. This will affect many people working in low paying and low skilled jobs, which will increase the expanding unemployment rates. This economic change will also affect our society with the rise in various criminal activities when people discover that they can't take care of themselves or feed their families the way they used to.

## What can we do to protect ourselves?

Now that we have a basic understanding about some of the potential problems and situations that can affect us all, what can we do secure ourselves in the future? These changes can dramatically affect our economy and our livelihood if we don't get on top of them right away and begin to make plans for them both. The question is? What can we do to protect ourselves, our income, and our livelihood and get prepared for these future changes? There are three things we can do right now.

1. **Planning ahead-** If you understand that a problem exists or an issue is on the rise and coming soon, should you wait around for it and see what happens? Or should you prepare yourself and your family for what's coming before it happens, so you're not affected by the issues when the economic crash or the financial meltdown happens?

   If you're working on a job right now and a major stock market crash were to happen tomorrow, would your job be in jeopardy, or would it be safe? If not? What can you do today to secure your financial future and come out on the other side of the stock market crash with a stable income? This is something every person who has a job right now should be thinking about while times are good. You should plan ahead. You don't want to be caught off guard if a stock market crash actually happens, so get your finances in order starting now.

2. **Start thinking globally today-** The business world has gone global because of the Internet and the digital economy. The days are gone when a business only operated within the borders of its own country.

With the creation of the Internet, all companies can now sell and manage their business online globally. Take some time to think about a business idea that you can run and operate globally with a worldwide appeal that will allow you to sell all over the planet. There are so many individuals who have become millionaires overnight because of the Internet. These individuals offer goods and services that are enjoyed by customers from all around the world. Think carefully about your ideas and plan for your next new business with a global mindset, and you just might become the next internet millionaire yourself.

3. **Control your cash flow and emergency funds**- Everyone should create an emergency fund with at least six months of living expenses saved up in the bank just in case of a financial hardship. You need to be prepared if an actual emergency situation were to happen to you or your family today. All financial planners will tell you that you must setup an emergency fund right away if you happen to consult with them. You want to save the necessary funds for you and your family just in case of an actual emergency, so that the economic burden will not crush you financially. It's very important to be prepared for any financial disruption you may have to face if you lose your job, or if your car were to break down tomorrow, you want to be ready for anything. We are currently living in very uncertain times right now, so to prepare for this uncertainty; you should have at least six months of living expenses saved up and ready to go at any given moment if this is even possible for you.

In closing, you must realize that we are all living in an uncertain world right now, and no one can predict the future. It's far better to prepare yourself for everything rather than preparing for nothing at all. If something were to happen suddenly, you do not want to be crushed or devastated by an economic downturn that you could have prevented and planned for before it happened. Start today, protecting your economy and get properly protected.

## CHAPTER 7

# CONTROL YOUR DEBT TO INCREASE YOUR WEALTH

E veryone who has out of control finances hates being in debt. There are various reasons why so many Americans and individuals worldwide seem to find themselves struggling to get out of debt and financial slavery. For most Americans, debt is a heavy burden that overshadows them within their daily lives and constantly appears to be draining their bank accounts and their pocketbook consuming most of their financial resources.

**Did you know that America is a nation that runs on debt? Currently, about 80% of Americans have some debt level that they are struggling with daily such as: expensive mortgages, credit card debt and student loans.** Many Americans also struggle to pay on their monthly bills, expensive auto loans, and medical debts. Because all of these debts which are crushing so many people, it's causing a huge increase in financial bankruptcies across all age groups, including many retirees and the millennial generation.

**What is good debt?** Good debt is a tool used by corporations and businesses to increase their strategic financial positions and business revenue. This is when a business person can borrow a bank loan or get money from a venture capital firm to expand and grow their business. It can be used to hire more employees, increasing the company's production of its products and services.

Good debt can even be used to purchase new and increased equipment needed to expand and grow the company as they see fit.

**How the business owner uses good debt-** The very smart business person is someone who knows and understands the value of what good debt is and views is it as a means of **"Leverage."** Debt for the smart business person is looked at as nothing more than borrowing a financial resource for an activity that they can leverage later on to increase their company's growth, assets, and profits.

**What is bad debt?** Bad debt is usually the kind of debt you see most consumers struggling with every month. This is usually an unearned financial resource or money borrowed from a financial institution or bank that's used incorrectly by a consumer. If not used properly, it can crush your finances and can cause a shortfall within your business if you own one. Using debt incorrectly can mean employee layoffs, company downsizing, and even possibly your business going into bankruptcy. The most common types of bad debt are expensive car loans, credit cards, personal loans, and payday loans. When you have an abundance of bad debt, it can usually affect your ability to create and increase your financial wealth and investment savings. This is because you are spending most of your financial resources paying back the monthly bills and interest payment for the bad debts.

## Steps to help you get out of debt

1. **Increase your personal income potential-** Try to discover new ways to increase your income potential if possible. This can be challenging for many people living with bad debt because the debt is so high, and the monthly interest payments are killing their bank account. The average American who has a job with a set paycheck will have a hard time paying off their bad debts because of the high-interest payments on that debt. The increasing cost and expensive charges continue to consume most of their extra money each

month. Try to find a second job or side business that you can start to raise the extra cash you need to pay off your bad debts sooner. This can give you the relief you're looking for to help you get out of debt and on the path of financial security.

2. **Think outside the box-** Thinking outside the box is simply trying something different other than what you have always done before. You can try something new which can be completed after you have finished working on your current job. You could consider getting a second job, possibly delivering pizza? Or you could start driving for Uber or Lyft to earn a second income, which would help you pay off your debts even faster. You can try to learn a new skill-set that would allow you to become a consultant and increase your earnings even faster, which would allow you to pay off your debts. Any of these ideas could help you improve your income potential, allowing you to double up or triple up on your debt payments and get you out of debt a lot sooner.

3. **Budgeting your way to success-** The absolute best and systematic way to get out from under bad debt is to create a realistic budget. Take some time to create a realistic budget that you can live within and make sure it includes your entire monthly income and every bill and expense that you owe. You would like to tackle the debt with the highest price tag and interest rate first and foremost. The reason for you doing this is because that high-priced bill is costing you the most money every single month, which makes it even harder to get out of debt in the first place. Next, you want to take on the next most expensive debt that you have with the second-highest interest rate to start bringing it down as quickly as you can to be paid off. Eventually, you will be in a position where you can get all of your debts down to a zero balance.

4. **Celebrate your success-** Once you're in a position to where you can pay off the first bad debt down to a zero balance, then you should take some time to celebrate your success. You want to do this as a way of encouraging yourself so you can learn to appreciate the progress that you are making in the process of taking control over your financial future. Celebrate your wins as often as you can when you meet a goal. Some words of caution, please do not celebrate your success by getting into more of the same bad debts.

In closing, no one enjoys being in financial debt. If you happen to find yourself in this tough situation, you must work on a plan to get the debts paid down as quickly as you can. Never allow yourself to be in debt ever again if you can prevent it. Celebrate your financial success and your financial freedom whenever you can and never let debt take control over your life again.

CHAPTER 8

# HOW TO SAVE MORE MONEY THAN YOU SPEND
## THE 6 STEPS TO MAKE IT HAPPEN

Everyone knows by now that money doesn't grow on trees, and all dollars are earned from a job, a business or an investment that requires you to give up some of your time in exchange for wages. For most people, every dollar we earn comes from hard work and the long hours we spend on our jobs. Here are five of the main ways to get the money that we need to survive.

1. You inherit your money from a family member that has passed it on to you.
2. Someone donates or gifts you money because you are important or special to them.
3. You earn a monthly paycheck from the job or the company that you work for.
4. You earn your money from a successful business that you've started.
5. You make money from investing your way to success through the stock market.

There are several other ways to earn money that you need to survive, but some of them may be illegal, and you don't want to make a dollar this way.

If you want to be in a position to save and keep more of the money that you have earned from working on a job or managing a business, there are three important ways you can do this that we will now discuss.

1. One way to save more money if you have your own business already. You can create more revenue streams by adding new brands and developing new products and services that your customers will love and appreciate. This will generate extra revenue streams for you and maximize your product brand if done correctly. You can also increase your saving and wealth through financial investments you make that will increase in value and provide you with some dividends payouts.

2. If you're an employee with a company, you must create a workable budget to live within. You must carefully research additional investment opportunities known for increasing your wealth, such as real estate investment deals, stocks and bonds, mutual funds, ETF's, and **the various personal lending opportunities** that exist today. The right investment vehicle can increase your capital and your savings and get your money to work for you instead of you working for it.

3. Look for ways to save more of the money you currently earn through tax relief options that are written into law. Within the real estate market, there is the 1031 exchange when you are trying to upgrade to a larger home, which can save you money without the need to pay capital gains taxes. There are tax-deferred IRAs, tax-deferred mutual funds, and 529 programs in the investment world that will allow you to save a portion of your annual income. There are many corporate tax saving options in the business world to choose from and home-based business tax breaks available to you from your federal, state, and city government agencies that exist depending on where you reside.

## Control your spending habits

Most Americans have two big problems when it comes to saving more of their money and personal income let's review the following.

1. Many Americans live well outside of their financial means and spend more of their money on consumer goods, overpriced homes, luxury cars, and expensive jewelry than their income can support. Many Americans don't have the proper discipline and self-control over their spending habits regarding their finances that they should have. So many people choose to pay for these expensive and luxury items with credit cards that generally have very high-interest rates that can keep them in debt and struggling financially if they are not careful.

2. According to statistics, millions of Americans are slammed with financial debts that are very difficult for them to pay off. These debts are crushing them financially, and their bank accounts remain empty because of the many bills and debt payments they must make. These debts include expensive mortgages, auto loans, student loan debt, credit card debt, and personal loans. The average American household debt is around $132,529 as of January 2019.

If you want to position yourself to get out of debt and save more of the money you currently earn, you must take control over your spending habits and create a realistic budget for you and your family to live within. This budget must track every dollar of income you make and every dollar that is going out of your household on a monthly basis.

Let's now take a look at the (6) steps you can take to guarantee you will be able to save more money than you spend monthly.

1. **Create and follow a basic shopping list when you spend-** Whenever you must go shopping for yourself or your family, you should create a shopping list with only the items you need to purchase on it and nothing else. The one sure way to save more of the money you're already earning every month is only to buy those things you need on your shopping list. Most shopping malls and shopping centers are designed to get you, the consumer, to spend as much of your hard-earned money as you possibly can while you're there. If you go shopping without a list, it can be very easy for you to get distracted by all the sales items, specials, and discounts that the store owners and merchants present to you. Be very diligent with your shopping list when you must go shopping to save more of the money you worked so hard for.

2. **Monitor your recreational spending habits-** When discussing recreational spending, we're talking about spending money on things like vacations, going to the movies with your family, dining out at restaurants, partying while visiting local bars and night clubs and this will also includes purchasing video games and brand-new consumer electronics. Everyone who works hard needs a break and vacation from time to time, so recreational spending should be a part of your budget. Recreational spending can consume a huge part of the family budget in many American households if we don't use caution. You need to carefully monitor this area of your budget, along with the many other important responsibilities that you have going on in life, such as your budget for food, shelter, essential clothing, and transportation. You must make sure that the four essentials are at the top of the list regarding your household budget and your spending habits. Once you have these items listed and accounted for, then the recreational spending can be added to your monthly financial budget at that time.

3. **Try to make your purchase with cash-** Whenever possible, you should make as many of your purchases with cash as often as you can and try hard not to use the debt-driven credit cards that are readily available to you. Whenever you use your credit card to buy anything you want and don't use cash, there is an automatic monthly interest charge for every purchase you're making. When you pay on credit, you are essentially paying more than you need to for the same item you could have paid cash for. For credit cards, there are automatic interest charges that come with using the card frequently. Whenever people pay with cash, they tend to be a little more conservative with their spending habits because they can see the money leaving their wallets very quickly at the checkout stands. People think much harder about what they're buying when they pay with cash, and the question comes to mind do I need this item at this time? Or can this wait for a later time?

4. **Do you need the product brand names?** If you look very carefully whenever you're out doing some shopping, there are many different brands of products to choose from. The generic and off branded items you can purchase are often just as good as the expensive and well-known brands you see in the stores today. People are usually spending a lot more money than they need to for name brand products that work the same as the generic brands. Many people will only buy expensive name brand items just for showing off to their friends for have bragging rights. Do not live your life trying to impress other people who cannot do anything for you, and don't buy expensive things to ever impress anyone. Do not buy those expensive name brand items when you can save your extra money and purchase the generic brands that are just as good that so many people are raving about.

5. **Setup a real workable budget-** You need to setup a realistic budget that works for you and then track all of your spending habits to know where your money is coming from and exactly where it's

going. You should setup a budget that tracks every dollar that you're spending monthly. Your budget needs to cover the core items we've listed here and any other expenses that you may have.

- Shelter
- Food
- Clothing
- Transportation
- Utilities
- Entertainment
- Insurance

When you put your budget together, don't leave anything out; otherwise, it will fail and not work for you, and then you will be right back where you started in debt and struggling to pay the monthly bills.

6. **Always pay your bills on time-** The truth is no one really likes paying bills every month, but they must be paid, and you need to pay them early or on time. If every service that we required within our households were free, then there would be no need to worry about paying our bills on time. The fact is our housing, utilities, gas, and water bills are services that are provided to us by companies that distribute these services. Without these services, we wouldn't have a roof over our heads. No clean water. No lights or air conditioning wherever we currently live. Paying bills is a part of our lives whether we like it or not, and we must pay them on time, so you don't waste your money on late fees and reconnection fees that they will charge you if you're ever late.

In closing, if you want to save more of the money than you're spending every day, you may have to make some tough choices and sacrifice some of your unregulated spending habits. You must make every dollar that you earn count for something. You want to do this so your financial future will be bright and prosperous.

# CHAPTER 9

# GETTING YOUR BUDGET IN ORDER
## BREAKING THE DEBT CYCLE

D id you know there are millions of Americans that are struggling financially every day? Did you also know that the average American has about $12,687 in personal debt that they owe on? This debt includes credit card payments, car loans, student loans, and personal loans. Did you know that the national consumer debt for all Americans was at 14.3 trillion dollars by the first quarter of 2020?

Did you know there are more than 40 million Americans currently living in poverty in the USA? These impoverished Americans are those people who make less than $24,563 per year for a family of four. Did you also know that 58% of Americans have less than $1,000 in their personal savings accounts as of December of 2019?

The data, statistics, and facts regarding American's debt issues are staggering. Many Americans are in deep financial trouble, and for many of them, there is no end in sight in the foreseeable future due to the current tough economic times we are all living in today. Many people are working much harder and longer hours just to make ends meet, but their debts seem to be consuming all of their excess cash flow, and they are get stuck struggling financially all over again. Many of them end up right back where they started.

## The time is now to change the future

The only way for the average working-class American to get out of poverty and stay out is to manage their finances and their debts as quickly as they can and save as much of their income as they can. They need to do this, so they can invest in the future and build some personal wealth. To start with, you want to setup three different types of savings accounts to increase your financial wealth.

1.  **Setup a basic emergency savings account-** This account would be money you save for an emergency or a rainy-day fund. This would be money you don't touch and is only used for emergencies you may have to face. When you set this account up, you don't want to touch it if you can prevent it. You want to make sure you have easy access to the money just in case something unfortunate or an actual emergency were to happen. You could then quickly fix the issue and get it taken care of promptly.

2.  **An investment fund-** Your investment fund account will be used to grow and increase your financial investments to increase your wealth for the future. There are many different types of investment options to choose from. You want to consult with a Certified Financial Planner (CFP) or a Wealth Advisor to discover which investment vehicle is the best fit for you and your family. Here is a list of some popular options available.

    - Stocks and Bonds
    - Mutual Funds and ETF's
    - Real Estate
    - Hard assets like gold, silver, and platinum
    - Bit coin or digital currency

If you have some concerns about which investment choices you should make or which options would be the best for you and your family? Please consult with a professional to help you get the clarity you need to make the best and most educated decision based on your risk to reward ratio that you're willing to be exposed to.

3.  **A Living Fund-** A living fund is a basic account you will use to live on for your everyday expenses. You will use this account to pay for basic amenities, pay bills, and for your family entertainment purposes. This account will have the largest amount of money within it because of the rising cost of living and the basic cost of food items that continues to go up every other month. When funding this account, you must consider the cost of inflation increasing at about 3% annually for everything you purchase on a regular basis. You will need 50% to 60% of your monthly income going into this account if you want to live comfortably and maintain your current lifestyle.

## Living on the right budget for success

To be successful financially, you must create a workable budget to live within. All budgets begin with two things, planning and writing everything down on paper. When you create an account for you and your family, two important factors must go into the budget to make it practical. You will need to write down and track every dollar coming into your household and every dollar that's going out every month. Without this important information, you will never know exactly what's going on within your finances. When you start your budget, you must have a goal in mind of what you want to accomplish; otherwise, you will never get where you're trying to go financially. For a clearer understanding, a budget is simply a record directing your money on where you want it to go instead of wondering where it went.

Remember, money is always flowing from one place to another or from one set of hands to another. When you budget your money, you are being proactive with it, and you're making things happen financially that work in your favor, and you are not allowing things to happen without your knowing about it.

## Creating a budget that works

1. **Follow the money by tracking your spending habits-** The first step to developing a great budget is to track your income and expenses for at least one month, whether using a smart phone app, computer program, or old-fashioned pen and paper. Be sure to record every expense and every purchase that's made within that month.

2. **Make savings contributions automatically** into your bank account even though every budget scenario may be different. Allocate at least 10% of your earnings toward your savings account using direct deposit to pay yourself first.

3. **Define your spending and priorities-** At least 35% of your earnings should set aside for housing and utility costs. Homeowners can often increase that percentage since principal mortgage payments are already a form of forced savings, and the mortgage interest they pay is tax-deductible.

4. **Pay with cash as often as you can-** Once you have determined how much money to set aside for saving, spending, and investing? It's time to make those numbers stick. Using credit cards and debit cards make it all too easy to overspend on consumer goods and services. Most consumers should implement a strict policy of paying with cash for groceries, clothes, vacations, and nonessential items if possible.

5. **Strategically pay down expensive debts-** You will never get ahead in life if you don't also implement a plan to pay down your debts. Interest payments made to credit cards cost you big and deny you the ability to apply that money toward savings for the future or even for entertainment for you and your family. So, pay down expensive debts as quickly as you can.

6. **Building up a safety net-** No matter what your debt situation is? You should begin saving for a rainy day immediately. Financial planners recommend setting aside 3 to 6 months' worth of living expenses for an emergency fund in case of a job loss, illness, or an unexpected bill.

7. **Live within your means-** Learning to live within your means is a simple matter of spending less than you make every month. For most consumers, this means cutting back on unnecessary expenditures that you don't need. It doesn't mean doing without.

## How to create a budget that works

Now, it's time to create your budget; let's look at a basic budget so you can understand what it looks like. Your goal is to account for every dollar that came in and budget each dollar down to zero dollars before you ever get paid. Being proactive with this approach, you'll want to create this budget and have everything figured out even before you get paid. You can start by putting your total monthly income at the top of the budget, and then underneath that, you will want to write down every single household expense for the entire month.

Next, let's look at an example of a simple but effective budget you can use as a guide to creating your own.

Remember, when you create your budget, be proactive and honest with yourself and your situation; otherwise, the budget is worthless. The budget is your lifeline to keeping control over your family's finances for now and into the future.

## Saving your way to success

It's very important to setup specific amounts of your income to maintain all of these accounts so you can reach your planned goals.

- 15% should be saved for your savings account.
- 25% should be saved for investments and retirement accounts.
- 60% should be saved for living and entertainment expenses.

Is it possible to somehow cut your living expenses down even lower? If so, then you'll be able to increase your savings and investment funds to maximize future returns when it's time for you to retire and call it quits from the world of working. Whatever money you get from your paycheck, take it, and divide it into the three accounts you have setup. Remember, you must be consistent month after month, and when you do this, you will see your accounts and your income increase just as you'll see your debts decrease, which is right where you want to be.

In closing, to overcome the world of debt that so many Americans and individuals worldwide are suffering from, you must change your saving and spending habits immediately. Start by creating a workable budget that you and your family can live within. Next, you will want to setup the three accounts we've talked about in this chapter and begin to move your money into each account according to what we have discussed as quickly as you can. Finally, be consistent by monitoring your spending habits, and over time you will see your income and savings increasing, and this is exactly where you want to be for now and into the future.

# CHAPTER 10

# AVOIDING BANKRUPTCY & HOW TO MAINTAIN YOUR FINANCES

A voiding bankruptcy should be something you should attempt to do at all costs. There is a high level of uncertainty within the economy that we're all living within currently. If you happen to ever be in a position where you find yourself financially bankrupt, the first thing you need to understand is that your life isn't over. Bankruptcy can also be a means of starting all over again. There are many people who must file for bankruptcy because they are in financial trouble, but they need to understand it's not that they have a terrible money problem as much as it may be that they are suffering from a lack of financial management skills. They also may be suffering from a lack of investment knowledge which is their real financial problem.

**Learn how to change your mind-set with your finances-** First, once you take enough time to address the problem with your lack of financial expertise and investing abilities, the money troubles will quickly vanish, and bankruptcy will be off the table for you. There are numerous working-class Americans who are not very successful at handling their finances and budgeting, and they are looking to fix their financial issues by tossing more monetary resources at it. When you do this, you're essentially gambling with the money you have, trying to solve your overall financial illiteracy issues. For many Americans who approach their finances this way, the money problem still doesn't get resolved. They still have a financial problem that they must live with until they get the proper financial education and investment skills to properly manage their money.

The fact is money problems are not solved by throwing more money at the problem itself. These financial problems are solved by increasing your financial knowledge, investment education, and learning as much as you can about how money works and how to invest whatever you make from your job or the business that you own.

**Learning what it takes to overcome financial problems-** People in high-paying jobs like Doctors, Lawyers, Accountants, and Engineers don't generally have the same financial problems that the average working-class person does, holding a regular 9 to 5 job. When you're in a unique, highly skilled position, you can increase and negotiate your income and wages with your employer more frequently, unlike what the regular employees can do. The higher the skill-set you possess, the more money you can potentially command and demand for yourself. In fact, this means these individuals who have these types of skills will never have to suffer from financial issues and money problems that so many working-class people have to deal with.

## Increasing your education from home without an expensive college

Going to college isn't the only option available to you. Some people will say: **"I can't afford to go to college; it's way too expensive?"** This may be true, but you're in luck; the average finance and business startup book at www. amazon.com can cost you $20 or less. These resources are readily available to you to read and study to change your financial situation for the better practically over-night. Below we have a list of some of the best finance books and web links for those who want to learn quickly and transition into a better financial life for their future.

## The resources -www.amazon.com

https://www.amazon.com/Rich-Dad-Poor-Teach-Middle

https://www.amazon.com/Rich-Dads-Guide-Investing-Invest

https://www.amazon.com/Rich-Dads-CASHFLOW-QuadrantFinancial

https://www.amazon.com/Total-Money-Makeover-Classic-Financial

https://www.amazon.com/Dave-Ramseys-Complete-GuideMoney

https://www.amazon.com/Soldier-Finance-Charge-InvestFuture

https://www.amazon.com/Intelligent-Investor-Definitive-InvestingEssentials

https://www.amazon.com/Investing-QuickStart-Guide-SimplifiedSuccessfully

## Financial Web Sites

https://www.m1finance.com - Free automated investing. M1 Finance empowers you to manage your money and build wealth with ease.

https://tradegenius.co -Learn to Trade and Make Money Nearly Every Day with The BEST Stock Market &Crypto Currency Training Programs Online!

https://www.fxcm.com/markets/forex/what-is-forex - Take a closer look at forex trading, and you may find some exciting trading opportunities unavailable with other investments.

https://www.babypips.com - The beginner's guide to FX trading, NEWS, TRADING, EDUCATION https://www.betterment.com - Our mission is to help our customers maximize their money. Whether you're new to investing or a seasoned pro, Betterment does what is right for you and your money. Our retirement recommendations could increase returns by 1.61% compared to those of the typical investor.

https://fundrise.com - Unlock a new world of real estate investing. You can invest your money, according to your goals, in a portfolio filled with dozens of real estate projects — each one carefully handpicked and proactively developed to grow your net worth.

https://www.robinhood.com - Invest Commission-Free Invest in stocks, ETFs, options, and crypto currencies, all commission-free, right from your phone or desktop.

https://www.firstrade.com - Brokerage Account. Build your family's wealth with an Individual or Joint brokerage account.

https://www.webull.com - Webull Financial LLC. Invest Smart · Trade Free

In conclusion, if you're struggling financially and trying to avoid bankruptcy, it's possible that you don't have a major money problem at all. But, it's more likely that you're missing out on some very important financial education that you are currently striving to learn. To start changing this situation, you need to get the correct financial information from the right sources. Once you can increase your knowledge, you'll see the difference that the training can make in your life and take more control over your financial future.

# CHAPTER 11

# THE COMING ECONOMIC COLLAPSE & HOW TO PREPARE YOURSELF

## Understanding the American economy and the turbulent times ahead

W arning! The global economy will have some turbulent times ahead, so prepare yourself. According to economists and the many reports that have been written recently, there is another economic crash coming to the U.S. and the global economy very soon. If you're paying any attention at all to the stock market, you've seen some of the turbulent ups and downs that have been affecting the Dow Jones Index, the Nasdaq, and the S&P 500. There are times when the U.S. economy is doing great, and then there are times when it's not doing so great at all. This is due to financial fluctuations and the unpredictable quarterly projections of the U.S economy and also the various stock market indexes that can negatively affect the overall economy. These financial fluctuations and quarterly projections can also have a negative or positive effect on Americans Gross Domestic Product (GDP) results. There are many other economic, financial, corporate business, and government policy issues that can affect the American economy. The ups and downs within the stock market are typical cycles that happen when the economy is unpredictable.

# Taking a look at the hundred-year history of economic collapse in America

- **The Great Depression-** The great depression of 1933 devastated the United States for more than ten years. GDP fell at this time by up to (29%), and the unemployment rate peaked at (25%) by the time the economy balanced itself back out with a ton of government intervention.

- **The 1973 OPEC Embargo-** The OPEC oil embargo caused increased inflation and a recession that contracted the economy by (4.8%) and unemployment then went up to (9%) when President Richard Nixon then took the U.S. dollar off the gold standard at that time.

- **The 1981 Recession-** At the time, increasing and high-interest rates were used to control rising inflation, and the economy decreased by (8%) as a result of the turbulent times. The unemployment rate had risen above (10.8%) by December of 1982, which affected many working-class Americans.

- **The 1989 Savings and Loan Crisis-** In 1989, several unethical bankers created this crisis when they teamed up with (5) different senators to crush the bank regulators so they couldn't be investigated once they were found out. The savings & loan crisis resulted in more than 1,000 bank closures, and the unemployment rate increased by (7.8%) at the time. The entire U.S. economy needed a $126 billion-dollar bailout to fix the issues caused by the unethical bankers.

- **September 11, 2001-** The 9/11 Attacks on the World Trade Centers in New York caused a 6-day closure of the NYSE, which caused a (617.70-point) drop in Dow Jones Industrial Average. The resulting Dow drop extended until 2003, and unemployment increased by (6.3%). The subsequent war on terror added an additional $2 Trillion to the U.S. National Debt.

- **The 2008 Financial Crisis-** The 2008 financial crisis was one of the worst crises in American history. This crisis was almost as bad as the great depression was in its time. The Dow fell by (770 points) when it started, and Presidents Bush and President Obama both injected ($700 Billion and $836 Billion) separately into the economy to reverse the decline. The housing prices started falling, and mortgage defaults began to rise at this time. The lenders had allowed too many people to take out sub-prime loans, which sparked the crisis.

## The future of global warming and other important factors you need to understand.

In an article of March of 2019, The Federal Reserve warned us of another economic crisis that may be coming soon due to the effects of global warming and the extreme weather patterns that are affecting farmers and utility companies around the country.

You can read a whole lot more about this important information in this interesting article: https://www.frbsf.org/economic-research/publications/economic-letter/2019/march/modeling-financial-crises/

Many cities in America have been hit hard by global warming. Some have even been devastated by the out of control wildfires, powerful hurricanes, tornados, and cold super storms they have had to deal with in recent years. Many states all over the U.S. constantly get affected every year by these powerful forces of nature that can crush their environment and wipe them out financially. In the future, we must contend with nature, which can dramatically affect the economy, but many other factors can seriously affect the American economy as well. They include the rise in WIFI (5G) technologies and Artificial Intelligence (AI). These technologies will be a challenge for many American workers who work in low paying jobs and the various minimum wage sectors of the American economy that will replace human personnel with robots very shortly.

## The future change factors that you need to be aware of.

- **The rise in E-commerce and online stores-** If you've been paying any attention at all, you will notice many brick and mortar stores are closing their doors every day. Stores such as: Macy's, Sears, and JC Penny's and there are many others. Many of these brick and mortar stores cannot compete with the online shopping convenience that so many people enjoy from their cell phones, tablets, and from their home computers. The brick and mortar stores will not survive within the digital age of online shopping and E-commerce stores like www.Amazon.com and www.Walmart.com. These brick and mortar merchants will need to adjust their business strategy and move a portion of their business into the cloud if they are going to survive in the future. As more and more people move to online shopping, the layoffs of thousands of employees who work at brick and mortar stores will begin to impact the U.S. economy negatively.

- **The rise in automation and artificial intelligence (AI)** - Robots and automation are on the rise in the U.S. and worldwide. There is an increase in robotic technologies and automated systems such as automated kiosks and self-driving cars that you're starting to see more commonly now. These changes will have an economic impact on millions of American workers and factory workers worldwide who didn't have to contend with robots for their jobs. Once these automated kiosks, robotic cars, and automated trucking industries are fully operational, this will have a major effect on taxi drivers, truck drivers, Uber drivers, and Lyft drivers who make a living transporting people and merchandise around from place to place.

- **The decrease in demand for automobiles:** -There has been a decrease in demand for automobiles in the U.S. today.

https://www.cnbc.com/2019/03/26/us-auto-sales-are-falling-and-cars-are-more-expensive-than-ever.html

https://exclusive.multibriefs.com/content/auto-industry-expected-to-experience-significant-decrease-in-demand-but-the/transportation-technology-automotive

In 2019 alone, the U.S. auto sales decreased by (2%) to (16.9) million cars sold, and it's estimated that the automotive sales industry is going to decrease again next year, down to (16.3) million cars sold. They estimate that by 2021 the demand for cars will be down to (15.1) million cars sold if the current trends continue in their showing pattern. This trend is transforming the millennial generation's attitudes, who are gradually utilizing other options, with the advent of companies such as: Uber, Lyft, and Turo. They are opting out and not wanting to find a vehicle of their own in the big urban cities across America. Many young people cannot afford the high cost of purchasing, maintaining, and registering these new and very expensive vehicles any longer when the jobs they are working for are not giving them steady pay raises and pay increases.

- **The decrease in demand for homeownership-** Many young people today are not buying homes just like the previous generations before them did.

https://www.investopedia.com/news/real-reasons-millennials-arent-buying-homes

There are many different reasons for this trend in the low home sales market within the millennial generation. Many of them cannot afford to purchase an expensive home on their limited income, working on their typical minimum wage-paying jobs. The other main reason for this is that many young people don't want the hassle of the homeowner mortgage payments, property taxes, home maintenance, and the rising insurance cost to have a roof over their heads. With the high cost of living today, the increasing student loan debts, and the various consumer debts that so many young people have, they are opting to stay at home and live with their parents until a later date in life. Many young people often choose to reside with roommates and their peers in apartments instead of paying for an extravagant house. They are doing this so that they can save the extra money they have earned from their minimum wage jobs that so many of them must work until they graduate from college.

- **The rise in student loan debt-** As of September of 2019, ($45) million Americans have over ($1.5) trillion dollars worth of student loan debt that they currently owe. Many poor and working-class American students cannot afford college outright, so they must take out government and student loans to get a decent education for a better life and a better paying job when they graduate. For most of them, when they graduate, they'll probably get an entry-level corporate job and will spend the next 20 to 25 years of their lives paying back the debt owed from the student loans they took out to attend college in the first place. The school loan process in America is a system that so many people, unfortunately, have to resort to because they honestly cannot afford to pay to go to these expensive colleges. The cost of education has gone up higher than inflation, around 3% annually year over year. Most working-class students who must take out student loans to pay for college it can be very tough for them because they generally have menial employment that pays them low wages without regular salary increases.

- **Having no emergency cash-flow-** Did you know that more than (50%) of American families are living paycheck to paycheck? Did you also know that (60%) Americans do not have $1,000 saved up in the bank if an emergency were to happen to them? For a large portion of the U.S. population, if an emergency or an economic crisis were to happen to them, they would be financially crushed. Many Americans are not prepared to survive an economic crisis or an economic collapse if one were to happen today. It's very important to start putting some money aside just in case an emergency were to happen to you today. You do not want to be surprised, especially if you can prevent it.

- **No retirement savings for many Americans-** Did you know that the average American has only $96,000 saved for retirement today? Did you also know that the average millennial under 35 years of age has only $13,000 saved for retirement? The financial experts say that by the age of 65, the average American should have at least $1,000,000 plus saved for retirement. Unfortunately, most of them only have around $100,000 saved for retirement at this time.

  **Social Security is running out of money-** Did you know that Social Security benefits are on track to be reduced by 2035. This is said to happen at its current pace unless the U.S. Government decides to do something about it. Medicare Insurance is said to run out of money by the year 2026 at its current pace if no one does anything to change it.

  **Baby Boomers-** The baby boomer generation is becoming eligible for social security benefits everyday by 10,000 persons per day, which is a huge drain on today's social security system. There are 77 Million Baby Boomers born between 1946 and 1964. This amount of people can take large chunks of the social security savings benefits out of the system that has to be paid for by those people still working on their jobs today.

## What is the solution to these potential issues?

As you can see, many different factors and issues can affect us financially within this economy. What should we all be doing about it right now?

1. Learn all that you can about saving more money, investing in the stock market, and managing your finances. You do not want to get caught off guard if an economic crisis or economic collapse were to happen tomorrow. You want to take complete ownership over your financial future.

2. Learn how to supplement your income by starting your own business or creating an E-commerce store online that can generate some extra income for you and your family regularly.

3. Pay off your debts as quickly as you can, and take full control over your consumer and credit card spending habits. If you don't take control of your spending habits, they will take control of you.

4. Try to buy some hard assets- hard assets include: gold, silver, platinum, and other precious metals that hold their value over time and have been the backup for paper (Fiat) money for more than 5,000 years. Hard assets represent real wealth, unlike fiat paper money that can lose its value over-night. If there is a sudden shift in the stock market, and no one has confidence in the system any longer, your fiat dollars can instantly become worthless.

5. Purchase real estate that can generate you some regular monthly passive income. You may even want to rent out a room in your own home for some extra income if you have the room available? This is a sure way to supplement your income with a home you already own in your possession.

In closing, no one can predict the future. While we are currently in a deadly crisis at this time in the United States (Covid 19), it's very important that we all understand the different factors that can affect each of us economically. We must all develop a financial plan for ourselves and the life of our families just in case an economic crisis or economic collapses were to happen to us tomorrow.

# CHAPTER 12

# REEVALUATING WHAT YOUR SCHOOL TEACHERS HAVE TAUGHT YOU

## EMPLOYEES OF THE U.S. DEPARTMENT OF EDUCATION

Everyone born in the United States by law must attend a public or private school from age 5 through ages 16. If your children are not in school, either public or private, the parents of that child can be fined or worse put behind bars. The law of compulsory education within the U.S. school system is compulsory for all children ages 5 to 16.

### Your school teachers are the guides and educators to your future.

All children and teenage students depend on their teachers to educate, teach, and motivate them with the necessary knowledge, education, and skills to help them become more intelligent and successful in their lives. When these students get the proper schooling and education, the hope is that they will be skilled enough to get a job or start a business within a field that they will enjoy that can pay them enough money to sustain their lives and support a family someday.

## School teachers - The intelligent employees, not the business owner or entrepreneur?

Your school teachers and the principal of the school you attended while in your youth were all employees of the U.S. Department of Education. This government agency mandates the curriculum that every public school must teach to every student in attendance. Every teacher at every public school within the U.S. is an employee of The U.S. Department of Education, and they are required to follow the government mandate, which is handed down to them from their superiors that must be followed and adhered to. All public-school teachers are delivered what should and what shouldn't be taught in schools to their students by someone in authority over them, and there are many courses that we must learn from them that have no real value or bearing on the future of our livelihood.

## The knowledge you should have been taught that wasn't made a priority while you were in school.

- **Most people are working for someone else for their own survival-** Every person who works for someone else on a job works for a business or a corporation that employs them. Without a job or the opportunity to run your own business or invest your money, you cannot survive in this world, which requires money for everything you need and desire. The only way around this process is if you happen to be born into a wealthy family that has setup up a living trust with financial resources already available to you. The other rare option is if you happen to live off the grid or be someone who has their own land and grows their own food, which provides them with everything they need to survive.

**The lack of business skills and business knowledge that many suffer from-** Since most businesses provide the general products and services that we all need to survive in our lives, shouldn't business skills have been one of the most important classes we all should have learned while in grade school? This could have been a game-changer for so many Americans if they only understood the value of business ownership, business financing, and business operations. The job option could have been a backup plan for those people who just didn't want to start their own business or for those individuals who didn't have the drive that it takes to create, run and manage their own company.

- **The lack of financial skills and monetary education that is needed-** I am sure you're well aware that everything we need and use in life requires money or financial capital to obtain or get access to.

1. Your residence cost money. Wherever you live or the home you currently own requires constant money to stay there and maintain.

2. The food you eat is not free. Whatever food you eat or groceries you happen to buy comes at a cost and requires money to purchase unless you grow your own.

3. Transportation has a cost. Whatever car you drive or transportation you use requires money to fill with gas, paying annual registration cost, smog checks, and maintenance services.

4. If you decide to have a family, there is an insurance cost, housing cost, clothing cost, a cost for activities, and a cost to send your children to college someday.

5. It costs you to be entertained and go on vacation whenever you desire to. If you ever decide to go on a vacation, they can cost thousands of dollars, depending on what options you choose for yourself and your family.

6. There is a cost to retire at the end of your working career. Money taken out of your paycheck from your job all the years that you've worked is stored up as a retirement payment so that when you're elderly and cannot work any longer, there is money available to help you pay your bills and live.

7. There is a cost even at death. You cannot die and leave this earth without the cost of a funeral ceremony. This cost can be expensive, something like $10,000-$20,000 or an inexpensive $650 cremation ceremony if you happen to be someone who doesn't have much money available.

As you can see, everything in life requires money or financial resources to access, so why wasn't financial management skills the second most important set of classes we should have been taught while in school?

- **The importance of learning real-life and personal communication skills-** Personal communication skills consist of basic things you should have been taught at home with your parents. These skills pertain to everyday living and communication with other people and having an open mind regarding those individuals who grew up differently than you did. Many children have come from broken homes or orphaned children who never had any parents teach them any type of life or communication skills. It would have been great while we were forced to go get our compulsory education that they considered life and communication skills a priority for all children to learn and understand. These skills could have helped so many children who come from broken homes manage their lives in a much better way, and it could have helped many of them develop the ability to take back control over the challenging conditions they have come from. These skills consist of the following.

1. Communication and interpersonal relationship skills
2. Creative thinking and decision-making skills
3. Basic cooking and self reliance skills.
4. How to balance a checkbook and pay bills on time.
5. How to maintain and run a household.
6. Basic budgeting skills and money management.
7. How to raise a child on a budget if you decide to have one.
8. Basic automobile and home maintenance skills

These are some of the most common skills that every young person should have been taught while in school, which would have prepared them to be successful in the real world that we live in. Think about how much better off we all could have been if we were fully educated and trained within the different areas we mentioned above. Everything we're discussing here is a skill that most of us honestly need to learn and understand. Unfortunately, many of these classes may have been electives if they were even available to us at all, and they were not the focus classes that so many people could have benefited from while in grade school.

- **Training in personal relationships and getting along with others-** Did you know that 50% of marriages in the U.S. end in a Divorce? Do you know what the top 3 reasons for the high divorce rate are in the U.S.?

1. **Money and finance issues**
2. **Infidelity and trust issues**
3. **Domestic abuse and violence issues**

How much better off could our relationships be if we were all educated and trained in grade school about how to get along with other people who are very different from us? What if we learned how to have more compassion for people who grew up in a different environment than we did? Personal relationship skills would have come in handy to teach many young people about different types of options and solutions when dealing with bullying or how to deal with someone who is displaying some type of superiority complex behavior. Some people have no concept or understanding about how to get along with others that are different from themselves. There are many people who respond to other individuals that they don't understand with anger and bitterness, and they don't even try to understand them. Instances like this are where personal relationship skills could have come into play to help these individuals have a broader understanding of the many different races of people that exist on the earth.

## The education in the life of wealthy children

The public school system has mainly been designed to educate children with just enough knowledge to prepare them for the job market and to be employed to work for someone else other than themselves. Many children born into wealthy families have had the opportunity to go to private or Ivy League schools where they are taught to be business owners, bankers, doctors, lawyers, and engineers.

They are also taught about the power of managing their finances, investing their money, and how to build personal wealth for the future. The wealthy remain in this state because they have learned how to increase their financial assets so that their money can now work for them and not them spending their entire life working for money. Working on a job for money is something we're taught within the public school system, and it's not what many of the wealthy children are taught in the private and Ivy League schools that they attended.

## Having a realistic understanding of our reality

In reality, the public-school system is designed to prepare its student to get jobs and become good hard working employees by working for someone else to make a living. They don't spend much time teaching us how we can work for ourselves and be independent of a job to make our living and survive.

We all go to school to learn the curriculum that they teach us, and then when we graduate, we go out into the job market, get a job and work for a company or a business to earn a paycheck for livelihood. The hope is that we can earn enough money from working our jobs to pay our way through life and possibly raise a family on our salaries. Working on a job usually provides us with just enough money to keep our bills and debts paid, and then one day, when we have hopefully saved up enough money to retire we can enjoy our golden years.

In closing, remember every teacher within the public school system are paid employees that all work for the U.S. Department of Education. This government agency oversees and sets the mandate for all public schools within the United States. Public school teachers can only teach us what they are told to teach by their boss. Therefore, many students lack the necessary business knowledge, financial awareness, personal growth, and relationship skills that we have discussed within this chapter. You must take ownership over your own life and educate yourself with the necessary information to best sustain and support the lifestyle that you really want to live. Do not expect to learn this valuable information from your school teachers; their bosses may not even allow it.

---

# CHAPTER 13

# THE CREATIVE MIND VS. THE EDUCATED MIND

Within this chapter we will discuss the difference between the two powerful mindsets that it takes to create, run, and operate a successful business. The first type of mindset that we will review is the creative mindset, and then we will assess the mind of the educated person. We will determine if one mindset is better than the other when running a successful business. Or should you have a little bit of both the creative and the educated mind to manage and run your business successfully?

## The Creative Mind

According to the dictionary definition, creativity is the use of the imagination or original ideas in the production of artistic works. Here are some other names for creativity.

- Inventiveness
- Imagination
- Innovation
- Originality
- Vision
- Ingenuity

These are just a few of the other names or titles given to people who show creative behavior or creative thinking. Let's now look at some very successful millionaires and billionaires known for being creative and innovative within their business models that never even graduated from a college university.

- **Michael Dell- of Dell Computers- <u>www.dell.com</u>, his net worth is 20.9 Billion**
- **Steve Jobs- of Apple Computers- <u>www.apple.com</u>, his net worth was 10 Billion while he was alive.**
- **Bill Gates- of Microsoft- <u>www.microsoft.com</u>, His net worth is 103.8 Billion**
- **Mark Zuckerberg- of Face book- <u>www.facebook.com</u>, his net worth is 75.5 Billion**
- **Even Williams- of Twitter – <u>www.twitter.com</u>, his net worth is 2.5 Billion**
- **Larry Ellison- of Oracle- <u>www.oracle.com</u>, his net worth is 71.6 Billion**
- **Jan Koum- of What App- <u>www.whatsapp.com</u>, his net worth is 10.1 Billion**
- **Travis Kalanick- of Uber- <u>www.uber.com</u>, his net worth is 5.4 Billion**
- **John Mackey- of Wholefoods- <u>www.wholefoodmarket.com</u>, his net worth is 75 Million**
- **Julian Asange- of Wiki-leaks- <u>www.wikileaks.com</u>, his net worth is 500 Thousand**

This is just a small list of some very well known and very successful individuals who have dropped out of college to start up their dream businesses. Each of these individuals pursued an important and elaborate career choice that included financial wealth for them over the need to graduate from a college university that would have only provide them with an academic and paper credential. A degree is nothing more than a piece of paper that proves you have some level of knowledge within a specific field of training. Degrees by themselves do not generate any real life-changing revenue for its holder it's just a piece of paper that acknowledges your education and level of studies. You still need to get a job or career path that pays you some real money to pay back the expensive loans that you took out to go to school in the first place. The only thing most of us have at our graduation ceremony is a paper credential, some added knowledge, and a huge debt in the form of government loans and grants. All the famous businessmen and entrepreneurs that we have just mentioned above all dropped out of college. They used their creative abilities to develop massive wealth for themselves and some very amazing and powerful companies we all know and love. As you can see, being very creative plays a huge part in any business's success because creativity is where most of the product ideas begin to take shape in the minds of the creative person. You have to develop your creative ideas and bring them to life if you want to be successful.

## The Educated Mind

The dictionary definition of the educated mind results from or having a good education or highly trained in a specific field. Here are some other names for someone who is highly educated.

- Knowledgeable
- Well informed
- Intellectually aware
- Learned

An educated mind is anyone who has gained knowledge, skills, and training from a formal learning institution like a college, a university, or a vocational training center or from experience from reading books and training themselves. Education is very important and critical for many of the various highly specialized career choices. Careers such as: doctors, lawyers, accountants, and engineers require highly specialized training and skills from a formal learning institution for you to be successful at it. You must get the right type of education and training for many highly specialized career choices, and there are no shortcuts to your success when you decide to go down these career paths.

## The creative mind or the educated mind you choose, which one is better for your business?

**Creativity-** There are so many great businesses that exist today because the founders were very creative or someone within the company was very creative. The creative person had an amazing and creative idea that they wanted to bring to the market. Once they started the business, millions of people came to love and admire the product and services that these businesses offered. Having creative ideas is why many of these businesses are so very successful even today. Businesses like the following are great examples of what we're talking about when it comes to creativity.

- www.facebook.com
- www.youtube.com
- www.twitter.com
- www.linkedin.com
- www.amazon.com
- www.uber.com

Through the creative person's brilliant mind is where most of the amazing ideas are born, developed, and brought to life. Creativity is necessary for new businesses to succeed in a global economy where there are so many different players. All the competition is striving to be at the top within the market place.

**Educated-** Every successful business that exists today operates by following a strategic business plan and marketing strategies that help the business grow, expand, and maintain its customer base. All successful businesses require someone who is well educated in business management, business operations, business finance, and marketing. Business education is the core knowledge; you need to start, operate, and maintain any business if you wish to be successful.

## There are no guarantees in the world of business

There are no guarantees with any business. Whether you're highly educated and even if you are very creative, neither one of these mindsets can guarantee that your business will be successful. It's very important to understand that the right idea with the right business plan can still fail if the idea's timing is wrong or off for some reason or another. Your great idea and amazing business plan can still fail if you start it when the market is going through a negative correction or the idea is not economically valid at the time.

Even when you're very creative and highly educated, or you have a bit of both, the other factor you need to consider that can affect your business's success is timing. When you bring your idea to the market, you must do it at the right time for the right niche market; if you don't calculate this carefully, it can unravel your idea and your business model.

### Developing your talents

There are many people which are much more creative than others. Some people are much smarter and more educated than others are as well. It really doesn't matter whether you're more or less creative or highly educated than someone else. If you take some time to learn as much as you can about your craft and you develop your skill-set, you can become just as smart and creative as the next person.

Take some time to develop yourself and learn all you can about what it is that you're gifted at. Once you have gained the necessary knowledge and skills that you need to start, maintain, and operate your business. It will not matter what the next person is doing because you will have solidified your ideas and will be able to bring your business to life to serve your customers within your niche market.

In closing, all successful businesses have a combination of individuals with creative minds and highly educated people that it takes to run, operate, and maintain them. One mindset is not more important than the other, so invest heavily into your people so that you will have a good balance of both the creative and the educated minds for your business's success.

# CHAPTER 14

# CAREER CHOICES
## HOW TO CHOOSE THE RIGHT ONE

O ne of the most important decisions we all must make in life is choosing the right career path for our future. When you're young and you don't have a ton of life experience behind you, how do you know what the right career choice is for you?

Many people depending on the type of parents they had and the environment they were raised in, ultimately determined many of the choices and decisions that were made on their behalf until they were mature enough to make decisions for themselves. For so many children, their mother and father were a major influence on their career choice. Various other factors play a role in the career decisions for many young people, such as the available opportunities that may or may not be available to them in the city or state that they reside in.

## What the statistics have shown

The statistics tell us that people will make between 3 and 4 and up to 7 different career choices within their lifetime, depending on the sustainability of a specific career field. The advancements in technology and artificial intelligence will ultimately determine if your field will remain sustainable for many years to come. One important factor in making a career choice is to try and make sure you're looking at two important factors.

1. Make a career choice that has some longevity and a future. You want to make sure the career choice you decide on will be around for a long time, well into the future.
2. Make a career choice that pays very well that has regular pay increases. You need a real living wage with plenty of room for advancement in the future.

## Making the right career choice decision

To help you better understand the thousands of different career choices you can make, you can visit a career planner.

- www.careerplanner.com – This site has a list of over 12,000 careers to choose from, which include the following.
  1. Education requirements
  2. Job outlook
  3. Salaries
  4. Work environment
- www.thebalancecareers.com – Learn how to make a career choice when you're undecided. The Balance Careers makes navigating your career easy. It is home to experts who provide clear, practical advice on job searching, resume writing, salary negotiations, and other career planning topics.
- www.collegechoice.net – Go to this site to learn about the highest paying careers for college graduates today.

## Parental decisions that can affect your choices

As we mentioned at the beginning of this chapter, millions of young people grew up in households where their parents were making all of the important life and career decisions for their children. Sometimes these parents have even attempted to force their children into following a career path that they have wanted for that child, and it's not exactly what the child wanted to do for their own future. The unfortunate thing for these children is that when you're living in your parent's home and under their supervision, you may have to follow the rules and plans they have setup for you until you are old enough and knowledgeable enough to make your own decisions. It can work out great when both the parents and the children agree on what career path should be decided on for that child's future.

## How environmental circumstances can affect career decisions

For many of the children who grew up in working-class families or very low-income families within the U.S., they may not have had the option or the choices for various career paths available to others. This is partially due to coming from an environment that has limits regarding their family incomes and financial wealth that may not be available to them. There can be some great career choices for the struggling and working-class families that are available. The more expensive Ivy League schools and the very expensive universities might not be possible unless that child works very hard at getting good grades. Then they might receive a full-ride scholarship from one of these institutions.

If you find yourself in a position like so many American families who struggle with money and finances, there are other ways to achieve your goals and dreams and still make a great life for yourself.

- **The military option-** this includes joining the Army, Navy, Air Force, and Marines.
- **The community college option-** this is a pay as you go option that takes a bit longer but can still get you the results you desire.

- **Vocational trade school option-** Learn a vocational trade like becoming an Electrician, AC Technician, Auto Mechanic, or even a Carpenter.
- **Starting your own Business-** this option is the best one for those who cannot afford to go to college because even the college students, when they graduate, will need to start a business unless they plan on working in the corporate world.

## Discovering what works best for you

Many people will tell you to follow your dreams in life and do whatever you love to do. Realistically, you should follow after a good career choice first that can make you some money and generate you some personal income. Once you have saved up enough money over a period of time, you can then work on whatever it is that you love to do. The best career choice is the one where you're making an excellent income and doing something that you are completely passionate about.

In closing, choosing the right career is not always an easy thing to do when you're young, and you don't have much real-life experience behind you. Take some time to discover who you are as a person and what you love doing. Once you have researched this for yourself, you can evaluate some of the different career choices available to you and then decide which one would be the right fit.

# SECTION 2

## THE BUSINESS EMPOWERMENT TOOLS TO SUCCESS

# CHAPTER 15

# THE ENTREPRENEUR MINDSET
## THE 8 PILLARS OF SUCCESS

I f you ask most working-class Americas about the opportunity to start their own business today, they will tell you that they would love to start their own business and work for themselves. For many people, becoming an entrepreneur is a dream that they believe they want to start for the type of money they think they can make from it. Many of these same people don't understand that being in business is not an easy task, and it takes plenty of hard work, self-discipline, and long hours initially when you're trying to get it off the ground. Many entrepreneurs will tell you they have had many sleepless nights in the beginning when they were faced with some business and financial challenges affecting their company's startup.

Being in business for yourself is not a fantasy or dream; it takes some real determination and commitment and an amazing business plan if you think you're going to succeed. So, how do you know if you're truly ready to become an entrepreneur?

We will discuss the (8) critical pillars you must develop if you think you're ready to become the next successful entrepreneur.

1. **Developing natural optimism** —Are you someone who is constantly thinking about creative and inventive business ideas all the time? If the answer is yes, then when these creative ideas happen to present themselves to you, you must write them down so you can follow up on them later if you truly think it can be a money-making opportunity. Many entrepreneurs are very optimistic and creative individuals, and to be successful they must have a positive outlook and natural optimism, which is part of the creative process. This is very important in the process of starting your own business.

2. **Be willing to take on calculated risk** —There are risks in everything we do in life. The important thing we must do when assessing risk is to make sure it's calculated and accounted for as often as possible. Most of the very intelligent entrepreneurs use the probability factor or other risk factor formulas to account for the risks that may be involved in their businesses.

   **Probability Equation-** Formula for the probability of A and B (independent events): p (A and B) = p(A) * p(B). If the probability of one event doesn't affect the other, you have an independent event. All you do is multiply the probability of one by the probability of another.

   **Risk Equation-** There is a definition of risk by a formula: "risk = probability x loss. Risk = Likelihood x Severity."

3. **Taking action** — If you're an entrepreneur and have a great idea, you want to investigate the money-making potential of your idea very carefully. Still, you also want to start your idea with a business plan and bring it to life. All great ideas take timing, careful planning, and you must be willing to take the necessary action steps to achieve your projected goals as needed.

4. **Make it better than the competition** – if you're the type of person that will look at something and say to yourself, **"how can I make this product even better?"** Then you are someone who has the spirit of an entrepreneur within you. Do you have the knowledge and the ability to make a product or service better than the competition? Then you may be able to take the lead with your product idea and the market share of that business from your competitors. If your product or service is amazing, you may be able to even take their customers away from them with your much better brand and highly improved products and services.

5. **Become someone who thrives from challenges** – If you ask most people how they feel about challenges? They will tell you that they like things nice, easy and smooth in their lives. No one goes out into the world looking for challenges that they honestly desire to face. If you're someone who happens to enjoy a good challenge and can think your way through tough issues and tough scenarios, you may very well become a successful entrepreneur. Being in business for yourself can come with many challenges and hurdles you may need to overcome. The successful entrepreneur needs to think quickly and intelligently through each problem and challenge if they ever plan on succeeding within the business world.

6. **Looking for money-making opportunities** – The successful entrepreneur is constantly thinking of new ways to make more money and increase their wealth potential. You should always be on the lookout for new ways to get paid from business opportunities that you run across. You don't want to miss out on an opportunity to make money from a business venture whenever it appears to you. Sometimes you must be in the right place at the right time to take advantage of the new money-making opportunities, so always keep your eyes and your ears open for new opportunities when they present themselves.

7. **Your mind is always at work** – entrepreneurs don't waste much of their time focused on the small and trivial things in life or within their businesses. They generally, are highly focused individuals driven by empowering thoughts and new ideas, which can increase their business and wealth potential. Time is money for the entrepreneur, and since there are only 24 hours in a day to get things done, they choose to use their time very wisely. To truly be successful, you must have the right advisors around you and the right assistance and support to deal with the little trivial things so that you can concentrate on your business vision for the future.

8. **The fear of being average** – No one who is truly successful looks at anything that's considered average and desires it. They do not admire becoming an average person. Being average is the worst place that the entrepreneur ever wants to be in. All successful business people desire to be at the top their game or be as close to the top as possible. Successful entrepreneurs want to be the best, and most of them will not settle for anything less than the best for themselves and the future of their business.

In closing, if you learn all that you can about the (8) pillars of success that we have discussed within this chapter, you may be ready to become a successful entrepreneur. Being in business is not easy, and it takes some hard work, long hours, and a solid business plan if you want to be successful. You must apply your knowledge and the skills you have learned into your business idea, and at that time you will be on the road to success.

# CHAPTER 16

# THE TOP 7 RULES TO BUSINESS SUCCESS MADE SIMPLE

Every successful business starts with a great leader, some amazing products and services, and a complete business plan that accounts for the businesses daily operations and also projects for its future growth. The very successful businesses in operation today also require a dynamic management team and a solid business and marketing strategy that supersedes the competition. Suppose you want to know which businesses are doing it right. In that case, you can look at many of the top fortune 500 companies that are doing business within the U.S. These are the 500 biggest corporations in America that make billions of dollars every year because of four very important reasons.

- **They have a great leadership team that drives the corporate vision.**
- **They have a very dynamic management team that can develop and expand the business for future growth.**
- **They have excellent products or services that their customers love.**
- **They have a solid business plan that projects the company's future growth and business expansion.**

## Here are the top 7 golden rules for any business owner who wants to be successful in the digital economy.

1. **You must think outside the box-** Within the digital economy, you must rethink traditional methods for analyzing and assessing financial challenges that can affect your business expansion. You must develop comprehensive solutions to the various challenges you may have to deal with within the corporate business structure today. The fact is some issues may need some Out-Of-The-Box Thinking to be solved properly. The traditional methods of the past for solving problems sometimes don't work today because of the modern-day technical issues that are involved. The millennial generation and people who use technology in general understand that the modern day issues might be unique in scope and require a more advanced level of thinking to bring the problems into resolution. The Out-Of-The-Box thinker will need to assess a problem with a different approach than that of a traditional person. The new way going forward may have a much more creative or even a more radical solution to resolve the issue that no one ever even thought about.

   Many great leaders and business owners such as: Bill Gates, Steve Jobs, Elon Musk, Jeff Bezos, and Warren Buffet are all out of the box thinkers. They think very differently than most average people, which is why they are so successful. You can see this based on the success that they have all achieved and the wealth they have generated because of their amazing ideas and the products they have brought into existence, which were looked at as radical compared to what the norm was at that time.

2. **First-person to the finish line wins the race-** The person who crosses the finish line first, wins the race in any competitive sport or business venture that exist. In other words, **look for opportunities to make a difference within your industry and try to see what**

**others cannot see by forecasting into the future and be the first to cross the finish line.** Discover the niche' market that everyone else is missing out on and then fill in the gaps with your products, services, and your ideas that you may have. Once you find the open crack in the wall, you want to fill it with your ideas and be the first to get there or the first person to the finish line.

3.  **Diversity is a key component to success-** Within many successful businesses, there is usually some level of diversity within the various groups and teams that exist. Diversity can help in a company's successful direction for future growth. Diversity can come in many forms, for example when it comes to the number of men versus women within the organization to bring about various and diverse viewpoints. Many companies have diversity in the area of brainstorming for ideas. Diversity is very important regarding experiencing a number of foreigners who work within the organization that can bring about diverse cultural ideas to any business. Accepting diversity can bring about some unique viewpoints and perspectives of the world that no one in the organization may have thought about before, which can add value within your overall organization. Having different perspectives and ideas can help your business see problems and issues in unique ways that they didn't see before. These new perspectives can be very valuable because you can now understand the world and your customer base even better than you did before. Diversity can be very important in the areas of problem-solving for any organization that values its people.

4.  **Join the generosity club-** Once you're in business and you begin to see a certain level of success, your organization should try to give back to your community and become more generous in giving something back to your customers who spend their hard-earned money on your products and services. You want to be very generous and caring with your team members as well because without them,

how successful would your business even be. Your team members are very important to your business's success; they are the individuals working long hours and putting in the time to make sure that the products and services your company produces are getting out to your customers without any issues or delays. The big companies and those organizations known for being generous often see even more success than what was expected because of their giving spirit. Remember, no one wants to be around a tight-wad, and everyone loves a giving person or a generous, genuine, and authentic company in their giving efforts and concern for others.

5. **It would be best if you built the right team for success-** Building a big business or a very large corporation is not like being in business for yourself. There is much more involved when going corporate and hiring large groups of people to work with instead of hiring a single person. Large companies have multiple departments with many people in various positions that all work together for one common goal and vision, which is to expand and grow the organization to its maximum potential. To truly be successful in any industry, businesses need to acquire the right personnel within the right positions to make the business operate successfully. Once these individuals are in place, they should be allowed to use their skills, talents, and expertise to help the business expand and succeed. They should all work towards the same vision and mission statement for the success of that organization.

6. **Invest heavily in your team and your people-** Just like building the right team for your business's success, once you have the right people working within your organization. You should look carefully for those exceptional qualities within your team members, such as leadership skills and those individuals who show great Integrity. In addition to leadership skills and integrity, you must also look for those who people have perseverance abilities and

someone who has a sense of community skills and is a team player. An individual's perfect resume or the elite and prestigious school they went too doesn't always mean that this person is the right fit for your organization. It would help if you looked for exceptions to the given rules, and then you'll find those special talents within your team members necessary for a great organization. Once your team is established, you should invest heavily into them to ensure they have everything they need to be successful within your organization. By investing into your people, you will see their best and get the best from them when running and operating your business.

7. **Understand the value of your customers-** Every person who is in business for themselves should understand the value of their customers. Without them, there is no business at all. Since your customers are so important to you and your business's success, take some time to make them the top priority within your organization's plan for the future. You want to provide your customers with everything they need and exactly what they want to keep them happy. Remember, you're in business to provide products and services for them and not for yourself. Always try to customize and tailor your products and services to fit your customers' needs since they are the individuals spending their hard-earned dollars within your business. It would be best if you became a customer-oriented business, and then you will see the rewards coming back to you repeatedly through the profits you're making from them continuing to buy your products and services.

In closing, if you want to be successful in your business, you must understand the seven core golden rules we have just discussed within this chapter. Try to implement each of these ideas within your business model and then watch how successful your organization will become.

# CHAPTER 17

# THE 10 MILLIONAIRE SUCCESS HABITS FOR THE AVERAGE PERSON

The absolute best entrepreneurs that run amazing businesses generally are very good at creating new and exciting product ideas that they will try to bring to the market place. Many entrepreneurs spend their valuable time trying to develop their businesses to be successful. They try to discover and incorporate the right team members for building businesses that are poised to be great within the niche market that they serve. Many of them have a great understanding about how to acquire the best quality personnel, such as managers and directors, which will allow them to maximize their company's potential for its business success.

**If you're new to starting a business for yourself, you need to understand exactly what drives the intelligent entrepreneur. The primary question most of them ask is? "How can I make this product or service better than what it already is?"** Let's now look at some very important success habits of millionaires that you must understand.

1. **You must have a vision-** A vision is a clear picture and understanding that you have within your mind for your business that you want to bring to the market. When you have a vision regarding your ideas, you will see things very clearly whenever a problem or certain

challenges arise. You will quickly be able to develop some real solutions that can make your business operations much better within your company that's needed for future growth and development.

2. **Conquering and overcoming challenges-** In life we will all go through various problems and challenges that we must embrace and overcome. The big question is, when these problems and challenges show up for you, how will you get through them successfully? Many people choose the pity option whenever challenges happen to them. Then, there are others who will move into more dangerous behaviors like using drugs and drinking alcohol to hide and disguise their feelings when facing problems and challenges.

Some individuals can even become very violent and destructive whenever they are faced with challenges in their lives. None of these behaviors are very positive for you to embrace whenever problems and challenges arise, you must try a different approach with a more successful outcome. Whenever you're faced with a challenge in your life, try to see the problem very clearly and then develop a solution or multiple solutions that can bring the problem into resolution. If you absolutely cannot think of anything on your own, then try to consult with someone like an advisor that you trust and see what they would do regarding the problem you're facing. You can then try to implement their ideas over your issue to see if it helps and works in your favor.

3. **Taking the necessary action steps-** Taking action requires some analytical thinking and careful planning. You need to take the necessary action steps to produce the results that you want and expect for a particular problem or challenge you may be facing. After you decide what you want to commit to, you should begin researching and planning for the necessary action steps it will take to achieve your goals. If you're not certain or very sure about which action steps

you should take, you should then consult with an expert within your area of business that you're planning to operate from and get an expert opinion to make sure you're moving in the right direction.

4. **Learn how to leverage personnel talents-** There are various ways to leverage someone's talents and their skill-set to promote your products, services and your business. You must be very creative with this approach to acquiring talented individuals within your organization. You must understand that you can accomplish a lot with the right people on your team, so you need to learn how to carefully utilize other people's talents and skills to build your dream business. You need to first understand what is most important and matters the most to your team members and your customer base. You need to position yourself and your team of acquired talents as the experts within their respective fields and allow these individuals to do what they do best in building up your organization. Leveraging someone's talent will require that you pay them very well and that you give them every tool they need to be successful within their position.

5. **Taking on calculated risk-** There is some level of risks in everything that we do in life. We are at risk whenever we are driving in our cars going to work every day to earn a living. There is a risk whenever we fly on a plane from one destination to another. We can still encounter some risk when we are safely indoors at home with our family. In everything that we do, it all comes with some level of risk. You absolutely must take on some levels of calculated risks to gain any high level of success in life and in the world of business.

Within the business world, risk must be carefully calculated and assessed if you're going to engage in any process which requires it. You don't want to take on any risk without calculating the pros and cons of every decision that you make; if not, this risk could potentially destroy and break your business if you don't. You do not want to put your entire business and vision at the risk of losing it all because that risk was not carefully calculated.

6.  **Leadership skills are crucial for any business to be successful-When running a successful business; you must understand what it takes to be a great leader and manage your team members**. To get on the path of becoming a great leader, you must first develop leadership skills within your own personal life and within the life of your family. Once you assume leadership within yourself, you will clearly understand how to become a great leader within someone else's life. Great leaders must be honest and have integrity, and they absolutely must be able to inspire others within their organization. To do this successfully, they will need to have some excellent communication skills. Great leaders must also have excellent decision-making capabilities and some levels of creativity, innovation, and empathy for others to truly be successful at it. All great leaders must set an example for others to follow, and by doing this, these inspired individuals are the people who will develop the future vision for the company and will drive it up the road in the direction that will lead to its success.

7.  **Learn how to become a people person-** Typically, the people person is someone who is very approachable, likable, and has a deep concern for others in need. Becoming a people person means that you're open to others, including those individuals who are very different than you, these individuals may have a different background other than that of your own. Many people within our society like to talk about themselves, so the more interest you show in their lives, the more interest they will find within yours as well. Learning how to become a people person is essential in business success because you can get the best out of those individuals around you when they

know that you genuinely care and have concern for them. There is a saying the goes, **"People don't care what you know until they know how much you care."** Think about that the next time you meet someone new.

8. **Think big and plan big-** Did you know that the brainpower you use to think big takes the same amount of energy whenever you're thinking about the small things in life? So, why not think big when it comes to your vision, plans, and ideas for the future of your business since they both take the same amount of brainpower and energy.

   Whenever you start to think big and make your plans for the future, try to think about a (1) year goal, a (5) year goal, and even a (10) and up to (20) years out if you can.

   Think carefully about your ideas and how they will look in the future and beyond. You want to visualize your businesses' potential within each period of 1, 5, and 10 and even up to 20 years from now. This will help you to determine if your plans are on track with future industry changes and business innovations. Planning big and thinking big will help keep your business and your ideas relevant for the future and beyond.

9. **The value and importance of delegation-** Just like leveraging talent for your businesses success, delegation is tasking the smartest people within your organization with the work and the duties they are gifted at. You need to allow the people within your organization and the teams to lead and manage the various departments of your business that you're not so great at running yourself. You must empower them to succeed within their position by giving them all of the support they need. You can help them through focused mentorship, advanced management training, and regularly educating them on business innovations.

10. **Branding yourself-** Within the process of branding yourself, you must first create a company and a product brand that you're proud of that you're willing to stand behind and put your name behind with passion and conviction. You must make sure your brand represents you and your product lines very well. Your customers must love your brand and have a deep desire for it at all times. Whenever your customers think of you, they should be reminded of your brand, and they should be happy because your brand is so amazing. Branding yourself can take some time and energy to accomplish, and many times, some investment capital to make sure your products and services are the absolute best for your customer base.

In closing, we have just discussed the ten millionaire success habits that the average person needs to understand for their own business success. If you attempt to follow these ten very important steps, you are almost guaranteed to be successful. Each step comes directly from the most successful business owners and company leaders within the business world today.

## CHAPTER 18

# THE 7 THINGS THAT THE RICH BUY THAT THE POOR DON'T

To understand how the rich and the wealthy spend their money, you first need to understand the difference between what assets and liabilities are.

- **Asset** – Anything that pays you money or increases your wealth in value over time.
- **Liabilities-** Anything that costs you money and decreases your wealth in value over time.
- **The working poor-** Most of the working poor who only have a job working for someone else and not working for themselves, they generally, have many more <u>expenses</u> and <u>debts</u> (liabilities) than the wealthy people do. They need to quickly learn how to increase and get more (assets) into their investment portfolios. Most of the poor need to learn how to decrease their risk and take on fewer liabilities that keep them struggling financially on a daily basis.

## Understanding what the rich buy with their wealth

1. **The top priority for many wealthy people is buying any revenue-generating business or multiple businesses that generate residuals and profits** - Buying a revenue-generating business

is the number one asset that rich people invest their money into to maintain their wealthy status. Working for someone else on a job that so many Americans are trapped into doing will never make you rich; you will only be collecting a regular paycheck every month. You must take some of your earned income and invest it into a revenue-generating business opportunity that can eventually sustain you and your family for generations to come. This is what the wealthy do every day.

**You can visit some of these sites to learn about businesses you can purchase:**

https://www.franchisegator.com – Learn about many different franchises you can purchase with minimal capital needed at startup.
https://www.franchisedirect.com – Franchises you can buy for fewer than 25K. https://www.franchise.com – A ton of franchises you can start at great prices.
https://www.websiteclosers.com – One of the largest business brokerages in America.
https://woodbridgegrp.com – Brokers for buying and selling your business. https://www.businessbroker.net – Buy a business that works for you. https://www.bizbuysell.com – Buy any type of business that you are looking for.

2. **Investing heavily into real estate projects that provide residual income-** One of the most popular types of wealth-building assets of rich people is investing in huge real estate projects that generate residual income. Real estate ventures such as: multi-unit housing, apartments, shopping centers and shopping malls provide residual income and real estate sales. They also partner with very large corporations who build big structures like stadiums, hotels, and convention center spaces that generate monthly residual income. The wealth constantly look for deals that generate regular monthly

residual income. Everything we have just mentioned happens to be money-making assets that the wealthy are always heavily invested into.

**Take a look at some great places to start for the average person who wants to get involved in real estate projects.**

https://fundrise.com – Fund rise makes investing simple, allowing you to benefit from greater stability and higher potential returns.
https://www.jamestowninvest.com – Now you can add commercial real estate to a traditional stock and bond portfolio.
https://seniorlivingfund.com – Funding communities and investing in longevity.
https://diversyfund.com – Your financial future depends on your choices today.

3. **Investing into paper asset classes that increase in value-** Stocks and bonds, ETF's and mutual funds are very popular with the wealthy and they are heavily invested into these paper asset classes that they can purchase very easily. They look for assets which have a high rate of return and high dividend yields. You can quickly convert paper assets into cash if necessary, by liquidating them on the stock market exchanges that exist. The wealthy love paper assets because of their high liquidity value.

**Here are some places you can investigate to see if they have something that interests you when it involves paper asset classes.**

https://robinhood.com/us/en - Commission-free investing.
https://www.tdameritrade.com/home.page - TD Ameritrade commission-free trading.
https://www.webull.com – No commission on investing stocks.
https://www.m1finance.com – Smart money management.

https://www.acorns.com – helps you grow your money.
www.stash.com – changing your financial future.
www.betterment.com – Robo advisors for saving in the future.

4.  **Purchasing fine art and antique pieces worth millions of dollars-** Wealthy people love to purchase world famous paintings and expensive celebrity art work pieces. They also love to purchase expensive sculptures and antiques that are sometimes worth millions which will hold their value or increase in value over time. Celebrity art work and antiques are another asset class that can create liquid cash flow as needed for the owners of these types of expensive art pieces and antiques.

    **Take a look at some locations. You can purchase your fine art and antiques.**

    https://martinlawrence.com – Fine art collector and seller.
    https://kamelmennour.com – Top art dealer.
    https://www.ropac.net – Top art dealer.
    https://artsation.com/en - Top art dealer.
    https://www.ranker.com/list/list-of-famous-art-dealers/reference- Famous art dealers
    https://www.vanityfair.com/style/2019/03/duel-of-the-megadealers - Most famous art dealers.

5.  **Purchasing of classic cars and exotic automobiles-** Most rich people have a collection of original classic cars and expensive exotic vehicles worth millions of dollars. This way, they can drive them for pleasure or very easily sell these vehicles as needed at car auctions like Mecum whenever they want to and make a profit or liquidate them to extract some cash flow as they see fit.

    **Locations, you can get access to classic and exotic cars.**

    https://www.bonhams.com – Buy and sell your classic cars.

https://www.mecum.com - Buy and sell your classic cars.

https://classiccars.com- Buy and sell your classic cars.

https://www.hemmings.com/auctions - Buy and sell your classic cars.

https://www.barrett-jackson.com – Buy and sell your classic cars.

6. **The importance of owning intellectual property rights-** Intellectual properties are things such as: patents, product brands, and company trademarks that everyone is familiar with and loves. The wealthy like to get access to the patents and copyrights of prized materials and specialized processes that they can get their hands on and have the right to. This can make them millions or even billions of dollars that can be sold or licensed off to other people and large companies. Intellectual property rights are very popular because the rich can then license these products and brands and make a ton of money just by signing a Franchise agreement with a private individual or big corporate enterprise. This would be something like Pepsi, Starbucks, Disney, and many other companies with franchised products or licensed product brands that millions of people love and want to purchase.

**Take a look at some options for intellectual property brokers that can help you.**

https://www.interactivebrokers.com/en/home.php- Brokers

https://cascadesventures.com – Protecting your rights.

https://www.ast.com – Protecting your patent rights.

https://www.upcounsel.com – Helping with your legal patent issues.

http://www.iptrader.com – Firm help with all intellectual property needs.

7. **Purchasing hard assets and precious metals that hold their value over time-** Hard assets would include metals such as: gold, silver,

and platinum. Gold is the one hard asset that has always held its value throughout time and history. Gold has been one of the number one hard assets for over 5,000 years by many countries and dynasties that lived long ago. There are other very valuable hard assets like diamonds and rubies that are highly prized as well.

**Here are some sites where you can get access to precious metals for yourself.**

https://sdbullion.com – Purchase gold and silver with this broker.
https://www.moneymetals.com – Purchase gold and silver with this broker.
https://silvergoldbull.com – Purchase gold and silver with this broker.
https://bullionexchanges.com – Gold and silver broker-dealer.

**These are the top seven asset classes that the wealthy will purchase regularly that the poor do not, and this is one reason why the rich remain financially secure and at the top year after year.** For those who are not aware, there is also a bonus asset class that you need to understand that many people are not even aware of, which can make anyone wealthy with the right idea and a plan in place. Even if you're starting from ground zero and you don't have much money to start with, this bonus asset class can bring wealth and finances into your direction once you understand it. The 8th asset class we're talking about is called **Personal Branding.**

**Personal Branding-** Personal branding is simply making a name for yourself and focuses on building up your brand because you're the face of a product brand that everyone loves and needs. For this type of branding process to work in your favor, you must first control a large audience of people who respect and listen to you because of who you are or the brand that you represent. You must develop the ability to build up an audience just like many famous YouTube celebrities and the Face book gurus that exist today. You can make a ton of money in a short amount of time once you develop your brand and add value into the lives of the audience which you have their attention. This process can take some hard work and time investment into it to see the benefits. It's not an easy thing to do overnight. Once you brand yourself on any of the various social media platforms that exist with the attention of your audience, you will forever have them interacting with you as long as you continue to add amazing content and added value into their lives.

Personal branding is a type of asset class that takes careful planning and some valuable time to build it up. Once it's established, it can be one of the best opportunities for you to make money at because you can scale it as you see fit by adding more value into the lives of your audience. Anyone can succeed with personal branding by investing into themselves and being heavily invested into the audience that they hope to work and grow with.

In closing, now that you know the difference between what an asset and a liability are. You want to make sure that you get as many assets as you can, and you want to keep your liabilities at a minimum if possible. Take some time to learn as much as you can about the many different asset classes we have discussed within this chapter, and then try to get as many assets as you can afford. With the personal branding process, you want to build upon your own personal brand that your audience will love. If done properly, you might just become wealthy and become the next millionaire that the entire world is talking about.

## CHAPTER 19

# THE NEGOTIATION SKILLS THAT CAN CLOSE DEALS

The dictionary definition of negotiation is- The method by which people settle differences. It's also the process by which a compromise or agreement is reached while avoiding argument and dispute. The dictionary definition gives you an overview of what classic negotiations look like. In the business world, there is an art to negotiating business deals that you must understand if you're going to be successful at it.

## The three steps to a successful negotiation Process

The negotiation process consists of two or more parties coming to the table, presenting each of their sides of the business deal to exercise the best possible outcome that works in their favor.

- Whenever you're in a position of negotiating a business deal, one of the most important things you need to understand is the perspective of the person you're negotiating with. Take some time to examine where this person is coming from. Try to understand why this deal is important to the negotiator by getting inside his or her head. By doing this, you will be able to align your needs for the deal and the needs of the person you're negotiating with. Put yourself in their shoes and try to see the deal from their side. Try to see the deal's value as if it works in their favor as you would your own. This is a good thing for the future of negotiating deals with this client in the long-term.

## Always ask for more than you need

- Before you ever begin the negotiating process, you must know your limits. What are your lowest and maximum limits that you're willing to take to close this deal or walk away from it altogether? An example would be if you're looking to make $5,000 from a special deal that you're negotiating for, you want to set the maximum limit at say $8,000, which will give you some wiggle room to work with.

  If they don't agree with your price, you can negotiate it down to your actual minimal limit, which is $5,000 right where you wanted to be in the first place. If you happen to get the client to negotiate down to say $6,000, you now have a $1,000 bonus on top of your actual asking price. Remember, to always ask for more than you need; that way, you hit your mark every time in the negotiation process.

## Remove the blame if the deal goes negative

- There are times in the negotiation process where neither party may be able to come to a common agreement, and the deal breaks down and goes south. You don't want to hold the blame for a failed agreement. If the process breaks down, this can ruin business relationships. The way to handle this is by letting the negotiator know you will need to consult with your team members or your boss if the asking price doesn't work for you. This is a tool you can use to put the negotiator on notice so you can try to get an even better deal if necessary. Leverage the conversation by saying, **"Let me call my**

**boss or my team to consult with them based on this price you're asking for."** When you do this, understand that the deal can go either way in your favor or not in your favor. Try to negotiate even further by asking if they can do better than that. You will want to position yourself as someone who wants to make the deal work but, if the price cannot be agreed upon, it's your boss or your teammates that don't agree on the price and not you. By doing this, you are keeping the relationship intact with the negotiator and pushing the negotiation breakdown and disappointment off on others within your organization and not on yourself.

In closing, any deal you are in negotiations with, you need to try and understand the perspective of the person you're negotiating with and try to see the deal from their position and the value it will bring to them and their organization. Always ask for more than you need when possible. This is a classic strategy that has always worked for the most successful negotiators. Finally, never take the blame if the deal goes south. Always blame the breakdown on your boss or someone else within your organization if there is no final agreement. You never want to accept the responsibility of a failure if the negotiation process goes south, and a deal cannot be made. You want to look like the guy who is trying very hard to make the deal work but, it's your team members who are the ones who don't agree on the price of the deal. You don't want to look like the bad guy in any negotiation process ever, and you don't want to ruin the potential relationship you have developed with this organization. Push the blame off of a failed deal onto someone else within your organization, so you have the opportunity to do future deals with this individual and their organization.

# CHAPTER 20

# THE POWER OF NETWORKING WITH THE RIGHT PEOPLE

**A very powerful statement to understand about the power of networking is: It's not what you know that counts, but who you know that counts.**

**N**etworking with the right people- When networking is done properly with the right people, it can open the doors to some great business opportunities. It can also help you land some new clients for future business ventures you may want to be involved in.

If you want to form a new networking relationship with anyone, you need to show them the value and benefits you can bring into their lives in this new relationship. When you're starting out in the beginning, you don't want to have any unrealistic expectations when trying to make a new connection with your peers or a new group of people you're engaged with. You should establish a personable and trusting relationship first. Once this relationship is established and in place, only then will you have the opportunity to cultivate favors, requests, and other resources from that person or group of individuals.

Try to think of networking exactly like an investment opportunity. You must first invest something into the account for a specific period of time before you should ever expect to get anything from it. The relationship will take some time to grow and mature, and once the time is right, you can start extracting the wealth you have built up inside that investment.

The more credibility you have built up into the networking relationship, the more likely a person will trust you and want to build a valuable relationship with you.

- **Trust and values are very important-** Whenever someone starts trusting you or they already have trust in you, this is automatic value added into your relationship with that person. The important thing about trust is that it's based on personal integrity, so you must say what you mean and do what you say. This is what integrity is all about. Whenever someone trusts you because of your sincere integrity, this is where your value will naturally increase with that person. It's critical that you first and foremost gain a person's trust within a networking relationship in order for it to work out in your favor.

- **Showing a sincere interest in other people-** Whenever you have genuine care and concern about other people, they can see this attitude within you. They will naturally gravitate towards you because of their comfort level. There is a saying that goes, **"People don't care what you know until they know how much you care."** Take some time to understand a person's needs and concerns, understand their interest and their fears. Once you know these things about someone, and then try to find a way to add real value within each areas of that person's life. Whenever you do these things properly, you can watch your team, and your network of friends grows like crazy. You want to try very hard not to be a push-over or a fake person; people can read into that right away because they are not ignorant to deception. Try to let things grow naturally as it should be in the first place.

- **The value of mentorship-** Try to partner up and network with like-minded individuals that are trying to achieve the same type of goals that you are. Look for a mentor that can help lead you on the path you would like to be on; this way, you can exchange ideas and strategies to develop you personally and intellectually in business as you see fit. When joining a networking group of people with similar goals, it will allow you to be able to partner with them and help each other learn, grow, and develop to reach your maximum potential together.

In closing, the power of networking with other people with similar goals, dreams, and passions is very important within the business world and our society. This is very important within the current social media environment that we all live in today. To excel in the world of social media, you must be a pro at networking and creating the correct kind of social links. Even within the employment sector today, employers are looking at your networking and social media profiles to see what their potential prospects for hire are up to and how they are spending their time away from the job.

# CHAPTER 21

# THE POWER OF CLOSING THE SALE

## Understanding the shopping habits of consumers

Did you know that the way in which consumers make purchasing decisions is constantly changing? It's very important to continually reevaluate your sales strategies based on the consumers purchasing decisions and their current buying needs. Today, the consumer and the shoppers are highly informed with knowledge because of the introduction of the internet and all the information that is readily available to them. **Selling any product or service online requires a perfect balance between being empathetic and persuasive with your respective audience.**

To successfully close any type of sale or business deal, you must first know how to communicate with your audience on their level. Once you do this properly, you will then be able to close the deal by offering them the benefits and value of the product or service you're trying to sell to them. You must make sure that the offer is so compelling that they absolutely cannot refuse it no matter what it is.

**Empathy is huge in the consumer sales field,** and learning how to empathize with your customers and consider their needs or what pains them is crucial to your success. You will need them to see your product or service as a solution to their problem or pain points to make a sale. Remember, whatever you do, try to make sure you don't come off like a robot or like a car salesman with them ever. This is the fastest way to lose a good sale with a potential customer.

**Understanding the customer's pain points-** Most people are not buying products and services without a purpose. They are trying to buy a solution to a problem they are experiencing in their lives. **Most people are buying a solution to something they have a problem with.**

**Some examples would be:**

- **Whenever someone wants to buy a new pair of running shoes that they need.**
- **Or when someone is purchasing a new economical automobile.**
- **Or even when a family is purchasing a home, their needs change based on a growing or shrinking family size.**

As you can see from either of these scenarios, the problem, for example, with the customer who is buying a new pair of running shoes, is that this individual is looking for a comfortable running shoe that would work whenever they run on different types of surface terrains. The right type of shoe would be a very important factor for this purchasing customer.

The person looking for a new economical vehicle is probably someone who needs to save money due to the rising cost of fuel at the gas pump, so they want to go economical instead of purchasing a large gas-guzzling SUV.

In the scenario with the family who is purchasing a home, it would be dependent on the family's growth size, or the downsizing of the family will ultimately determine what solution they need to the problem they are facing. They need a larger home for a growing family or a smaller home for a shrinking family.

Within each of these scenarios, the consumers have a problem that they need to consider before they make a purchase, and they are looking for a solution to their problem or their pain point in the purchasing process.

## Understanding the key principle of hitting a customer's pain points in the sales process will take you far when communicating with them.

**Learn how to listen and ask the right questions-** You must learn how to listen carefully and ask the right questions to get the right answers for your customer's pain points or the problems they are currently experiencing. You must listen very carefully as they speak to you without ever interrupting them to get a clear picture of their needs. Once you completely understand their problems, then you can tailor your product or service as a solution to their pain point. Doing this will then allow you to drive the sales process home with ease.

## Problems are what drive the sales process, and not products or services.

The product or the service that you're selling is the tool to fix the customers problem or pain point that they are experiencing. Think of it like the hammer or the saw is the construction worker's tool to build a much-needed housing structure. The problem in the construction field is that everyone needs a place to live. The solution to this problem is that we need construction workers to build homes for people to live in with their families.

Most people are looking for an answer to their problems whenever they're making purchasing decisions. This is very important to remember when designing products and services for your customers to purchase from your business.

**How do you handle challenges when it comes to the sales process?** When it comes to challenges in the sales process, you will not get any objections or have any challenges with your products or services if you design them to meet your customers' needs. When you have empathy for your customers and tailor your product and services to be a solution to their problem or pain points, you will remove all challenges from the sales process completely. You must learn how to understand your customer's questions and what concerns they have, and you must be very proactive in your sales approach. The customer should already know what to expect from the product or service that you're selling and how it will be a solution for them.

## The top 6 sales questions to ask your clients when you're meeting with them that will get the deal closed.

1. What inspired you to meet with us today?
2. Can you help me understand exactly what we're trying to accomplish here today? What is your goal from the end of this meeting?
3. How is your life or financial situation today?
4. Where would you like to go with this transaction we're involved in today?
5. What problems are you having, and for how long have you had them?
6. If we can accomplish what you want today, what would that look like for you?

In conclusion, you must understand everything that we have discussed within this chapter if you want to gain the power over the sales process. You must always put the customer first and tailor your products and services to resolve your customer's pain points. If you master this process, you can make the sale with ease, and it will be a win for the both of you.

# CHAPTER 22

# THE POWER OF PERSUASION

T he dictionary definition of persuasion is- **The process of changing a person or group of people's attitude or behavior towards something different than what they wanted before.** This can be done using written or spoken words or even a combination of both.

## *What does being persuasive mean to you?*

To persuade anyone regarding something that you want them to, you must have that person's full attention. The persuader must have a sense of integrity and leadership skills if they ever think that they will be successful at convincing someone about anything other than what that person already believes.

Whenever you're in a position of power or a role of leadership over other individuals, and your position is one that many would like to be in themselves, the power of persuasion can come very easily. All that is required is your ability to clearly communicate your message to your subordinates and then lead them carefully down the path of success. This process can happen effortlessly as long as you have the full attention of your audience. The one thing the persuader has to be very careful of is convincing people to do things that will ultimately harm or cause that individual some type of pain. This is one of the fastest ways to lose your persuasive abilities in the lives of people who trust you.

## Persuasive power

**Every powerful entertainer, politician, world leader, big corporation, and even our parents are constantly trying to persuade us to lean their way in one way or another.** Think about the politicians in government today. They are always trying to persuade the masses of people that they are the right candidate for the political position they want to be in. They work very hard to persuade you to vote for them at the ballot box during election time. The big corporations are constantly trying to persuade us into buying their products and services by putting down their competitors, as if their products and services are of a lesser value than those they are trying to sell to you today. World leaders and powerful celebrities spend a lot of time trying to persuade us to believe in them, or belief in their ideas and what they want us to follow along with that will keep them in their positions of power.

## The persuasive power of our parents

Our parents have spent most of our lives trying to persuade us into doing whatever it is they want us to do on a daily basis when we're children living in their household. Most times, our parents are wonderful people, and they can persuade us in ways that are good for us that will lead us into a successful future with a positive outcome within our lives. In some cases, the parental persuasion is moving their child into a direction that's not healthy for them, which will ultimately have a disruptive and terrible outcome within their lives. Either way, we look at it; these are all forms of persuasion and persuasion tactics used on children living with their parents.

## Becoming more persuasive

**Once you have securely established yourself with your audience and have shown them that you have integrity, excellent communication skills, and great leadership qualities, it will become very easy for you to**

**persuade them.** They will see these powerful qualities within you, which will make persuading and convincing them in one way or another very simple, and it will come very naturally for you.

In closing, take some time to learn all that you can about the persuasive ideas we have discussed within this chapter, such as **integrity, leadership, and communication skills.** Once you have mastered them all, you will then be well on your way down the road to becoming a much more persuasive person.

## CHAPTER 23

# LEARN THE MOST POWERFUL PERSUASION TACTIC EVER

D id you know that one of the most powerful tools ever used in the world of business is the power of persuasion? Many individuals use the power of persuasion to gain a slight advantage over others when it comes to getting their way in the negotiation process and when negotiating business deals. It's very powerful whenever you're trying to convince others to lean your way on a particular subject that you want them to understand. There is an actual science in the study of psychology behind the power of persuasion and its effect on people. The number one type of persuasion that we will discuss in this chapter is called: **"Reciprocity"**

The dictionary definition of Reciprocity is- **The practice of exchanging things with others for mutual benefit.**

## The reciprocity principle

Reciprocity is one of the basics in the study of social psychology: **It says that we pay back what we receive from other people in many social situations.** To better understand it, if your coworker does you a favor while at work, you are more likely to return that favor to him or her whenever the opportunity permits. An example would be if you're out at lunch with your coworkers one day, and you buy lunch for them without them asking you to do so? The next time you go to lunch with them, they will remember your kind gesture and good deed and feel obligated to buy you lunch the next time. This process is called reciprocity. Give onto others, and it will be given to you.

In life and business, try to be the first person to do something nice and generous for others around you, and it is almost always guaranteed that the next time around, he or she will be more than happy to return the favor. The reciprocity principle works every time.

There is another similar concept to the reciprocity principle called **paying it forward**. This is an expression or act of providing the benefits of a good deed by repaying it to others instead of the original beneficiary.

Whenever you're trying to persuade other people through your reciprocity actions, the most important thing to remember is to provide the recipient with a good gesture that's useful, helpful, and beneficial to them. That way, it will be easily remembered the next time around. If done properly, the favor will come back two-fold to you because the reciprocity principle generally never fails.

## The selfish person

The only type of person that the reciprocity principle may not work on is the selfish individual. These people only think about themselves and will always put their needs and wants over everyone else's most of the time. If you happen to be around these people, you will see this behavior almost immediately. No one likes spending much time around selfish people because they can drain everyone's energy. If you find yourself in a situation where large groups of selfish people surround you, escape from them as quickly as you can. People who are very giving and love sharing with others have nothing in common with the selfish mindset. You don't want their selfish ways rubbing off on you and letting it destroy your reciprocity principles.

## In conclusion

Be the first person to go out of your way to help, support, and show kindness to other people before it's ever asked of you. Do not expect anything in return. Just do it because it's the right thing to do. The natural psychology of a kind gesture is that the person on the receiving end will feel obligated the next time around that the opportunity shows up and return the favor to you without hesitation.

# CHAPTER 24

# EMAIL MASTERY
## GETTING IT RIGHT THE FIRST TIME

I n the world of communication today with so many social media platforms, email is still one of the most powerful and most widely used ways of communicating with people when it comes to family & friends, business associates, and communicating with customers and clients for those individuals who are in business for themselves. The history of mail, in general, is to get a recipient to read and respond to an important letter or some important information that you need to inform them about whether you know them or not.

Today, not much has changed; all email is nothing more than an electronic version of the old stamp and envelope process humanity has been using for years. There are 11 email subject lines that we will discuss within this chapter that work which will get your emails opened, read, and responded to. Let's discuss them in further detail now.

## The modern email- Understanding the purpose of the subject line and the body.

The email subject line is meant to get your email opened by a recipient and read in simple terms. The email body should be offering your readers something worthy or very valuable, like some great information, a PDF document that is invaluable to your readers, or some type of downloadable document that they will need and may use.

## The frequency of your emails- how often should they be sent?

- Frequency can happen daily if, for example, you are a blogger with timely information that you need to communicate with your followers.
- Weekly emails may be for more product and service-based businesses that don't change very often. With weekly emails, you want to update your audience about your **"hot sales"** or **"specials"** that you may be running each week.
- Monthly emails may be for businesses or bloggers who would like to keep their clients, customers, or followers updated and informed regularly for things that are not as time-sensitive. These monthly emails could be more informative or educational.

Within this chapter of email mastery, we will inform you about email tactics that have worked successfully over the years from real experience and from entrepreneurs who have been sending out thousands of emails every month.

## Learning what not to do with your email subject lines

One of the biggest mistakes that many digital marketers, entrepreneurs, and average Joe's make is selling within the email subject line. It would help if you never tried to drive a sale home within the subject line of your email. This is exactly what an inexperienced salesperson will try to do when they are only driven by money and making profits. No one wants to be sold to, so what will happen is the reader will then delete your email right away. Now you have missed out on an opportunity to build a lasting and valuable relationship with your potential customers.

The email subject line is not designed to make a sale. The subject line's only purpose is **to get your readers to open the email itself because the subject line is so amazing or compelling to them.**

## Understanding the purpose of the email body

The true purpose of your email body is to excite, educate, and inform your readers about some invaluable information that you know about or that you have which the reader never knew before. Within your email body, you want to provide the readers with a link that takes them to your offer or multiple offers that you may have for them. You're trying to guide your readers to your call to action with the link within the body of your email.

## Understanding the 11 email subject lines that will work for you

We will now look at the 11 best email subject lines that will work and we will give you a clear understanding as to why they work. Let's look at the most popular types of email subject line types that will get your emails opened before we get into them.

- **The fear of missing out- No one wants to ever miss out on a great opportunity.**
- **Pain points- If you can solve a problem for someone, they will for sure open your emails.**
- **Vanity- Vanity is a great way to get your emails opened because people can be very vain and very into themselves.**
- **Curiosity- This is a great way to get your emails opened when people are very curious about specific subjects.**
- **Greed- Greed can get your emails opened when people think they can get more of something for less.**

- **Straight forward- When you're direct with your emails, many people will value the direct approach.**
- **The discovery and how to approach- People love discoveries and how to do something that they never knew before.**

Now that you have a basic overview of the different types of email subject lines that will get your emails opened, let's take a deeper look at the 11 that will get your readers to respond.

1. **Fear of missing out-** No one wants to miss out on a good deal or a great opportunity, so the fear of missing out will get emails opened and read quickly.

   **Subject line- Urgent you have one day to get this before its gone**

   _____

   **Subject line- Today only get this now before its gone or to late**

   _____

   **Subject line- This weekend only, watch this video before its gone**

   _____

2. **The love of vanity-** Many people are in love with themselves, and vanity works very well with them. Try to use the vanity subject lines to attract these types of individuals.

   **Subject line- Don't wear the style of 2019 get the latest at _____**
   **Subject line- Get it first here the age defying beauty secret to _**
   **Subject line- Check out the products that the celebrities are using _ today_**

3. **Taking action today-** With this subject line, you're getting your readers to make a decisive decision right now and to take some type of specific action.

   **Subject line- Get out ahead of everyone start on your _____**

Subject line- Flash sale! Get yours today _____

Subject line- Check out the new _____ you don't want to pass on this

Subject line- Get priority access to _____

4. **Hitting pain points-** No one ever enjoys pain, and people will avoid pain at all costs. Any type of pain point headline will work very well.

Subject line- Stop wasting your time with _____

Subject line- How to survive the next _____

Subject line- Stop wasting your money on _____

Subject line- Don't miss out on getting _____

5. **How to survive-** The idea behind this subject line is that you are creating a solution to a problem your readers are experiencing. If you have a solution to their issues, people will respond.

Subject line-How to survive bankruptcy _____

Subject line- How to survive a financial crisis _____

Subject line- How to survive Covid 19 _____

Subject line- How to deal with _____

Subject line- How to get past _____

6. **The biggest mistake-** The idea behind this subject line is to avoid something if you want the results that you're looking for. People like to avoid mistakes, so if you have a solution for them, they will read your emails.

Subject line- The biggest mistake that all parents make _____

Subject line- The biggest mistake to make with your kids _____

Subject line- The biggest mistake when purchasing a home _____

Subject line- The biggest mistake the banks never told you _____

7.  **The real secret to-** Everyone likes to be in the know about what's going on, and no one likes to feel left out. If you reveal a secret to something, you will naturally make people curious.

    **Subject line- The real secret to becoming wealthy** _____
    **Subject line- The real secret to success** _____
    **Subject line- The real secret to winning** _____
    **Subject line- The real secret to losing weight** _____

8.  **The fastest way to-** In the world today, everyone is looking for new ways to get things done more quickly. If you have the fastest way to get something done, then people will listen to you.

    **Subject line- The fastest way to becoming wealthy** _____
    **Subject line- The fastest way to losing weight** _____
    **Subject line- The fastest way to buy a car** _____

9.  **Here is a shortcut for-.** This subject line focuses on how you can provide your readers with a quick solution to a problem they are having and struggling with.

    **Subject line- Here is a shortcut for making money** _____
    **Subject line- Here is a shortcut for getting out of debt** _____
    **Subject line- Here is a shortcut for saving money** _____

10. **How I can or how I did-** With this subject line, you're trying to help your readers understand the specific steps you took to complete a goal or task. You're trying to show them something you have experienced before that will help them.

    **Subject line- How you can overcome my challenges with** \_\_\_\_\_
    **Subject line- How I did launch my first business** _____
    **Subject line- How I took control over my finances with** _____

11. **About yours?** - With this subject line, you're invoking curiosity in the minds of your readers. You're showing the reader that you know something that they don't understand about a specific subject.

**Subject line-About your children, be careful of _____**
**Subject line- About your business, let me show you how to _____**
**Subject line- About your life, I can show you how to _____**

In closing, email is still one of the most prized means of communication today, in the digital age of social media, texting, and smart phone communications. If you want to have a successful email marketing campaign, you need to understand every facet of the email process. Remember, the email subject line is used only for getting your email opened and read. The body is where you give your readers some very valuable and important information that they need or they can use to their own advantage. Following our email guidelines within this chapter, it will give you a head start and an advantage over other beginners who may not know how to get it right the first time.

# SECTION 3

## BUSINESS SUCCESS IN THE DIGITAL ECONOMY & THE GROWING TRENDS

# CHAPTER 25

# SUCCESSFULLY BUILDING YOUR WEB BUSINESS
## AN INTRODUCTION

**M**ost people in business today, already understand the importance of the internet and that internet marketing is incredibly important because they have a clear understand about how consumers make purchasing decisions within the digital economy. Since there are so many people searching for products and services online every day, you need an online presence that can be easily discovered via search engines and online browsers. Many analysts indicate that there are increasing numbers of consumers using the internet, social media, and online research tools to look up products, services and research prices before making a purchasing decision. Internet marketing enables you to build relationships with customers and potential prospects through personalized communication, moving away from direct marketing and television marketing.

The topics covered within this chapter, combined with some easy-to-follow tips and tricks, will make this section of *getting your business on track in the digital age* a perfect fit for your business. This section covers many things that you will use to build your web business and acts as a guide to your plans and decisions for a more successful future.

No matter your level of experience, you will find that this section will guide you through the entire web marketing process in a step-by-step manner and provides a comprehensive path to learn about the many web marketing topics you need to know about.

*Why should I use the internet for marketing? It's*
*where the entire world operates now.*

## Convenience

The internet enables you to be open for business 24 hours a day, seven days a week, without worrying about store opening hours. Offering your products and services on the internet is also very convenient for your customers. They can browse your online store at any time and place orders when it's convenient for them.

## Reaching your niche

By marketing on the internet, you can sell your goods and services in any part of the country or the world without setting up a local shop, increasing your target market. You can also build an export business without opening a network of distributors in different countries.

## Your cost is minimal

Marketing your products on the internet costs less than marketing them through a traditional brick and mortar retail store. You don't have the recurring costs of property rental and building maintenance. You can order materials based on the demand, which will keep your inventory costs very low.

## Personalization

Internet marketing enables you to personalize offers to your customers by building a profile of their purchasing history and preferences. You can track the web pages and product information of your potential prospects visit, and you can make targeted offers that lineup with their interests. The information available from tracking website visits can also provide data for planning cross-selling ideas and marketing campaigns so that you can increase the value of your sales.

## Building relationships

The internet provides an important platform for building relationships with your customers and increasing customer trust levels. When a customer has purchased a product from your store, you can begin the relationship process by sending them a follow-up email to confirm the transaction and thank your valuable customers. Emailing customers regularly with specials and personalized offers helps to maintain a close relationship with them and builds trust.

## Social media is king

In closing, internet marketing enables you to take advantage of the various social media platforms. Using social media for growing your business and brand are of the highest importance which allows you to expand your business exponentially. You can take advantage of this type of influence by incorporating social networking tools into your internet marketing campaigns, increasing your desired revenue streams.

# CHAPTER 26

# THE INTERNET BASIC STEPS TO SETTING UP YOUR WEB BUSINESS

## What you will learn in this section

- ➢ An overview of the internet marketing steps you need to understand
- ➢ Building a plan for your website success
- ➢ Understanding your customers and who they are
- ➢ Developing a defined goal for your website
- ➢ Developing a working promotional budget
- ➢ Knowing your development skills and when to get help
- ➢ Digital marketing the hottest business in the 21$^{st}$ century
- ➢ The absolute best ways to make money online

I f you're new to using the internet for business and you don't understand how it can help you succeed in your business, don't worry. This chapter has been created to simplify the web marketing process for you. This chapter is meant to help anyone who would like to setup an internet service or product business and be successful at it. We will start with a basic understanding of the internet marketing process, and then you can develop a realistic plan that will enable you to have internet business success.

# What you need to know about the internet marketing process

The absolute best way to succeed with an internet business is through a step-by-step process with measurable steps that you can control at all times.

## Step 1: The importance of controlling your information

The most current and relevant information is powerful on the internet. In reality, the internet is a worldwide information database that allows everyone to communicate, trade, and interact with each other daily. Suppose you're going to setup a business on the internet? In that case, you must understand that you need to be in complete control at all times over your accounts, data, and the information on your business; this includes:

- **All website and design files and your account information**
- **All web hosting & email accounts**
- **Your domain registration and login information**
- **Any online backup service accounts and other important information**

Get www.dashlane.com - Never forget another password by keeping track of all your passwords; this is very simple with dash lane's free password manager.

https://www.roboform.com – With the Robo form, you will never need to remember or type your passwords again.

https://www.lastpass.com – The last pass remembers all of your passwords across every device.

https://nordpass.com – Get rid of your password stress forever.

## Step 2: Creating your products and services for sale online

One of the biggest decisions you need to make within the marketing process is deciding on what products or services you're going to provide to the world within your niche market. What financial methods are you going to use to conduct and transact product sales and services? What distribution methods are you going to use to deliver your products and services to your customers?

Spend some extensive time answering the above questions, and once you come up with the answers, then you must implement your business plan to bring about your ideas to the market place.

## Step 3: Conveying a solution to a problem

Does your product or service offer a solution to your customer's problem? Does your product or service make your customers feel good about them? If your answer is yes to both questions, then chances are you will get them to buy from you. Most people are looking for answers to the problems they have, and they may come to your site for a solution if you have designed your products or services to meet your customer's needs. Adjust and develop your products and services to answer a need or a solution to your customer's problems, and you will have a higher conversion rate of potential buyers.

## Step 4: Building web traffic to your site

On the internet, you want to increase your web traffic and get as many visitors to your site as you possibly can. You can do many things to make this happen, such as social media marketing, press releases, podcasting, search engine optimization, and many more we will talk about in other chapters.

One of your most important jobs being online with a web business is to try many different avenues and decide which ones work best to draw traffic to your site within your specific marketing budget.

**For more information on getting more traffic to your website, visit:** https://www.wordstream.com/blog/ws/2014/08/14/increase-traffic-to-my-website

- **https://www.outbrain.com – Building your business with native ads.**
- **https://www.taboola.com – Reach your customers on websites they trust.**
- **https://www.searchberg.com – Get more traffic, more sales, and more calls.**

## Step 5: What level of expertise do you have in your field

Most people like to shop and visit web sites that they know very well and have a trust relationship with. For your products or services, are you the known expert within your field? The analysts say that the fastest way to become an expert in any given field is to create a Blog with your creative skills, deep understanding, and knowledge about a particular subject; for more information, visit the following:

- www.theblogpress.com/why-blogpress - Learn why you should be blogging
- https://wordpress.org – Word press is an open-source software you can use to create a beautiful website, blog, or app.
- https://www.tumblr.com - Tumblr is a place to express yourself, discover yourself, and bond over the stuff you love. It's where your interests will connect you with your people.
- www.blogger.com – Create a beautiful blog for free.

## Step 6: Creating an effective & dynamic team

At some point, after you have developed and marketed your products and services online, you may need some help and need to recruit people to help you promote your business. You don't want to miss out on one of the best opportunities on the web, letting others help you sell your products and services for you and increasing your revenue. One way to do this is through an affiliate program.

**Top affiliate programs for 2020**

- https://www.shareasale.com – Great for beginners.
- https://affiliate-program.amazon.com – Great for beginners.
- https://www.shopify.com/affiliates - Great for beginners.
- https://www.clickbank.com – Great for beginners.
- https://partnernetwork.ebay.com – Great for beginners.
- https://www.rakuten.com – Great for beginners.
- https://www.cj.com – Great for beginners.

## Step 7: The Joint Venture- A partner in your business growth

This process includes partnering up with another organization; a joint venture (JV) is a business arrangement in which two or more parties agree to pool their resources to accomplish a specific goal. You want to partner with someone who will recommend your product or service to a large group of people you otherwise could not reach yourself. Doing a (JV) with the right person or organization could result in thousands or even millions of potential sales to your business.

**Some joint venture firms you can look at.**

- https://www.ideapros.com – Gives you some options in the market place.
- https://www.smergers.com – Connecting you with real investors.

- https://flowcap.com – A joint venture firm.
- https://www.missioncap.com – A joint venture firm.

## The strategic steps in the marketing process

On the internet, there are millions of online businesses, large and small. Still, not all of them are successful for one reason or another. What you want to do for your business to succeed is to follow a strategic plan of action with measurable results. To do this, you may need to get help from other internet marketing experts or service companies that offer guarantees with their marketing services. In the process going forward, make sure you know your business very well and know when you need the help of an expert, which can move your business forward so you can gain the success you're looking for.

## Organizing your website game plan

For starters, you must know your capabilities as well as your customer base. Next, determine what your customers are willing to spend on your products or services to keep them coming back for more. Finally, define and create a daily and a monthly goal on how much product or inventory you can sell within a given time.

## The importance of your website

Your website is your public face to the world, and it should be very important to you. You need to know that through your face on the web, you have total control. You want to make sure that you're getting people excited and inspiring people through social media efforts to visit and explore your website and learn all about what products and services you have to offer.

Your website is the most essential and critical part of your business, the heart, and brain of your operation on the internet, including the following:

- **Website must be cost-effective:** You must know exactly how much your website will cost you and its daily operations. A brick and mortar store, on the other hand, has many out of the ordinary expenses which could blow out your costs, such as leaving the lights on all night, theft, damage, extra staff members, etc. With your online store, you can remain open 24 hours a day, seven days a week.
- **Easy to increase customers:** You can gain customers from around the world being online and even compete with the big boys in the game and possibly take some of their customers and market shares.
- **Producing great content:** You can publish a blog or video cast with some amazing content and information for your audience and viewers in an instant on the right social media platforms.
- **Understanding what the competition is doing:** You can use many online tools such as Google Analytics to discover what the competition is up to and see how things are working out for them.
- **Easy payment system:** With the shopping carts today, you can collect credit card data with ease, get paid, and deliver your products and services to the customer immediately.
- **Having no website means you're losing business:** If you don't have a website presence online, you're missing out on opportunities for customers to identify who you are and allowing them to spend money with you. Your website should appear as if you have a team dedicated exclusively to keeping your online presence strong, valid, and important.

## Determining who your target customers are and the competition

When setting up your site, one of the first things you need to do is identify who needs your products and services and who your direct competitors are. Knowing these two important factors is the key to your business success. Often many business owners and entrepreneurs do things backward by creating a product first. Then, they try to find a niche or direct market to sell too. The easiest way to develop a targeted customer strategy is to see what target market your competitors are selling too and go after the same group with your product or services.

1. **Human beings have different types of needs.** Human beings have different types of needs that can be categorized into five levels from the lowest to the highest:

   - **Physiological needs.**
   - **Safety needs.**
   - **Love and belonging needs.**
   - **Self-Esteem needs.**
   - **Self-Accomplishment needs.**

   Does your product or service satisfy one of the needs in this list?

2. **Who are your competitors?** Use the internet to research out the competition. An example would be if you're a shoe manufacturer, just Google shoemakers in your city or state to determine who, what, and how they connect to their customers, and if they are successful, you can attempt to mimic what they do.

3. **Find influential people in your niche market.** This traffic tip is a big deal. Unless you can describe your target customers as **"influential,"** your target audience isn't going to share your content. If they don't share your content, you're not going to increase the necessary traffic to your website.

4. **Audience measurement analysis.** Some companies analyze a businesses' market audience, and they will provide this data to you, sometimes it's free, and some have a fee. This data can help you assess what the competition is doing in numbers and other important data.

- Go to http://www.nielsen.com/us/en/solutions/measurement/online.html.
- Or you can go to www.quantcast.com.

You must understand your audience as completely as possible. The more information that you learn and understand about your audience, the more amazing and interesting content that you can create for them. Quant cast measures and provides the data that you need to know and understand about your audience like the back of your hand.

## Establishing your website goals and a working budget

Once you are for certain that you have a **"HOT"** or in-demand product or service, and then you will be ready for the next step in setting up and defining your goals for your website. Here are some questions you need to answer.

- What amount of money do you need to make weekly or monthly for your business to grow and become more successful?
- Have you determined and calculated how many customers or sales you need each week or per month based on the cost of your product or service that will generate the amount of revenue that you need?
- What are the net sales you need to generate to be profitable after all of your expenses are paid monthly?

## Measuring your financial objectives and goals

Did you know today that all of your financial calculations and revenues you wish to generate on a monthly or yearly basis can now be calculated with specific math formulas?

1. **Determine your desired annual gross revenue.** Decide how much money by the end of 12 months you would like to make for your

business. $100,000, $500,000, or even $1,000,000 you decide the amount for your business.

2. **Use the average sales value formula (ASV).** To calculate this, you take the total amount of dollars that you received for all purchases within a given time frame divided by the number of purchases made. Use this to help determine the number of sales you need in the future to reach any desired gross revenue. Divide net sales by the number of products sold during the period.

   • **For example, if net sales in a month were ($497,000) and (400) units were sold, the average selling price for all products was ($1,242).**

3. **Calculating the projected average daily sales.** To calculate this, here's what you need: Use (DR) for the desired revenue. (ASV) is the average sales value. And (NPY) is the number of sales per year: Divide your sales generated during the accounting period by the number of days in the period to calculate your average daily sales.

   • **In this example, divide your annual sales of ($497,000) by (365) to get ($1,361.64) in average daily sales.**

4. **Conversion rate and how to calculate it.** Knowing your conversion rate is a first step in understanding how your sales funnel performs and what marketing avenues are giving you the greatest return on investment (ROI). Once you have defined what conversions you want to track, you can calculate the conversion rate. For the purposes of the following example, let's understand a conversion sale. You can calculate your conversion rate like this: **Conversion Rate = Total Number of Sales/Number of Leads * 100**

   • **Example: Let's say you made (20) sales last month, and you had (100) inquiries/leads. Your sales to lead conversion rate** would be (20%). If you're tracking conversions from website leads, your formula looks like this: Conversion Rate = Total Number of Sales/Number of Unique Visitors * 100

- Example: If you made (20) sales in a month and you had (2,000) unique visitors to your site, your conversion rate would be (1%.)

5. **Visitation conversion formula.** To determine the number of visitors per month to meet your sales revenue goals, use this formula, **where (S) is the number of sales you need. (C) Is the conversion rate (which is a percentage). And (V) is the number of visitors you need per month to visit your website: Formula is (Sales / Conversion Rate = Visitors)**

- **Example: At ($40,000) per year this breaks down to ($3,333) per month/.01 = (333,333) visitors per month.**

## Some detailed insight for analyzing information & data

- **Calculable data-** By using a few formulas, you can predict or know the probability of a possible outcome and determine for the most part what kind of revenue your business will make over the coming months based on the expected traffic you can expect to generate.
- **Responsive data-** While monitoring your website traffic, you have an opportunity to see which way things are moving based on the direction of things. You can investigate why it's moving in this direction and make immediate changes as needed.
- **Verifiable data-** Understand that everything on the internet can be tested and changed at a moment's notice, so spend some time adjusting and tweaking your ideas to increase your prospective clients and increased conversion rates.

## Assessing your spending budget

Spend some time calculating how much capital you have available to increase the traffic to your website. This is very important for your overall operating budget process because it allows you to setup and create specific marketing projections based on calculated results. You need to figure out what percentage of your budget can be spent on your overall marketing strategies.

## Understanding your responsible limits and know when to get help

Most people who setup web-based businesses do it because they want to be their own boss and secure their financial futures. Running an internet business takes constant decision making and adjustments so you can stay ahead of the curve. To be successful, you will need some help, so think about these questions to help you decide how much you want to be involved in the day-to-day operations:

- What are you truly skilled or gifted at?
- What task should you contract out to a vendor?
- Who do you know that can advise in the decision-making process?
- Do you know where and what your weaknesses are?

In closing, everyone who has some level of success on the internet has either a team of advisors or a specific group of people with specialized skills that can help them move their vision forward, so take the some and invest in building a team for your business's future success.

# CHAPTER 27

# MAKING MONEY WITH YOUR INTERNET BUSINESS

**What you will learn in this chapter**

- ➤ **Determining what it takes to make money & sales online**
- ➤ **How to multiply your sales and financial success**
- ➤ **How to increase more visitor traffic, paid and free**
- ➤ **Learn how to build and develop a sales team**

**M**aking money on the internet is not always an easy task. Some people spend a ton of time trying to chase the money and never quite get to their financial goals, while others can make their money instantly and with ease.

When trying to make money online, the first thing you want to think about is what type of product or service do I have to offer the entire world that can either help someone? Or appeal to their passion and desires. In this chapter, we will introduce you to many different ways that you can make money online. We will introduce you to some tools and strategies to increase traffic, gain more visitors, and increase the amount of money you can make from your customers.

## Learn the many different ways to make revenue online

There are many different ways to make money online. The first thing that you need to realize is that the things that make the most money from internet traffic are the products and services that offer and deliver amazing amounts of value to the people making the purchases from your website. Here are some core money-making categories to understand.

- **Try to sell and marketing your product or services that you have already created.**
- **Affiliate income is super hot right now and promoting other people's products.**
- **Blogging- by creating E-books, training materials, and selling great content is very popular.**
- **Formulating visitor traffic for profit through creating custom ads is also a great money maker.**

## Try to sell your own products and services

Selling your own products or services online can be very profitable if you have a great product and market it well. The beauty of this is that all the money you make is yours to keep except for expenses, and now because you have created your own product or services, you get to have complete creative control over your ideas, and your growth potential can be exponential.

Here are some important rules for you to consider when you're trying to sell your own products and services online:

- **The fact is that information products are still a top seller online** – E-books and how-to information products are some of the easiest products to produce and make available to your customers. Suppose you have some specific knowledge or expertise in a particular area or field. In that case, you can transfer that knowledge onto a computer and make PDF Files available to everyone on the internet for a small price. This is a great way to make some easy money.

- **Audio and video production products–** There is an incredible opportunity to make excellent income from producing MP3's and video productions available to your customers. You want to produce recorded products that have great content and promotional value. Think on the lines of powerful educational information, product demonstrations, documentaries, and there are so many others; it just takes some imagination and creativity.

**Check out the following online video sources:**

- www.youtube.com
- www.vimeo.com
- https://www.metacafe.com
- https://www.dailymotion.com/us

- **Webinars and online training sessions –** Create your own webinars. If you're an expert in a particular field or specialize in a certain craft, why not take your knowledge to the web and train people on your computer while the audience views your presentation online? The cool thing about this is these can be recorded and sold later for profits now and into the future.

**Check out the following webinar sources:**

- www.freeconferencecall.com/webinar
- www.anymeeting.com/free-webinar-service
- https://easywebinar.com
- https://webinarninja.com
- https://demio.com
- www.webinarjam.com

- https://home.everwebinar.com/index
- https://clickmeeting.com

- **Create handmade products that sell** - There is nothing like selling your artwork or custom picture frames, or hand-made custom jewelry that is appealing to a wide range of customers online, so if you have an idea or product that you think will make people happy or feel-good you may want to test it out online. You never know what can happen unless you try. There are plenty of success stories you can read about on the internet.

**There are amazing benefits to selling handmade items online.**

- **Your business will be involved in selling products you're passionate about.**
- **You can work from home, on your own schedule.**
- **You can quickly change your product line whenever you want to.**
- **You can establish a loyal and repeat customer base and following.**
- **There are various sites and marketplaces where you can sell handmade products online.**

## Affiliate income by promoting other business products online

An affiliate product is an item that someone else produces, provides, and maintains. All you have to do is endorse the product and urge visitors to visit the company's website. The great thing about this is when someone purchases the product because of your recommendation; you get paid a sales fee.

**Let's look at how an affiliate program works.**

1. **How to find an affiliate product to endorse.** The first thing you must do is find an affiliate product that interests you or that you're willing to support; this can be something you truly believe in yourself; or it can be a hot trend you have noticed. Whatever the case, choose an affiliate product you think will pique interest, that could be a money maker.

   **How to find a good affiliate program?**

   - Search Google for an affiliate product or industry with **Affiliate Program** behind it
   - Use a popular and well know affiliate gathering service such as:
   - Commission Junction- http://www.cj.com
       - https://www.shareasale.com
       - https://affiliate-program.amazon.com
       - https://partnernetwork.ebay.com
       - https://www.clickbank.com

2. **Setup and promote the affiliate link-** Once you have found the perfect affiliate product to endorse, you will need to go to the company's website and setup your account information. Once you have the correct web link to promote, you drop it into your business or marketing emails and on your website. As customers click on the company link and make orders, you get paid! That's pretty much it.

## Blogging- by creating E-books and selling great content

Here is some information on how to make money from a blog: https://problogger.com/how-to-start-a-blog

1. Set up your blog online.
2. Start creating useful content and valuable information.
3. Get your blog off the ground and start finding readers in your Genre.
4. Build engagement with the readers that come to your blog.
5. Start making money from the readers you have through one or more of a variety of income possibilities and products you sell to them.

## 5 easy steps to start a blog

There are a few simple steps that you will need to complete to start your blog.

1. Choose your blogging platform.
2. Secure a domain name and get hosting in place with an internet host provider.
3. Configure your blog to be reader-friendly.
4. Design your blog with a great and easy layout.
5. Start creating useful content that serves your reader's interests and desires.

## Formulating visitor traffic into profit with internet Ads

If you can drive traffic or visitors to your website, you can turn that visitor traffic into profits for yourself. You can do this without any affiliate programs and even without selling your own products or services. Another name for this is called **"Monetizing,"** which simply means converting something into money.

- **Setting up Google Ad Sense-** This is one of the most popular ways today to monetize visitors that come to your site. https://www.google.com/adsense/start/how-it-works, there are four steps to follow, and you're in the money.

Be aware that although Google Ad Sense is a great tool, the main intention is to drive your traffic to other people's websites.

- **Banner Advertising** – When you embed an advertisement on a web page. It is intended to attract traffic to a website by linking to the website of the advertiser.
- **Cost per Click (CPC)** - With this type of advertising, it is used to direct traffic to websites, in which an advertiser pays a publisher (website owner) when visitors click on the Ad.
- **Cost per Action (CPA)** - This is an advertising model where the advertiser pays for a specified sale, click or form submitted back to them.

## The Internet Buying Process in Detail

The first thing you must have to be successful online is an amazing web presence, and once this is established, the next thing you must ensure is that you sell an amazing product or service that gets the attention of every visitor to your site. The most important part is setting up your actual buying process that closes the deal and gets you paid through the online transaction system that you have in place.

In this next section, we will walk you through the online transaction components and offer pointers to ensure that the customers who buy your products or services have a simple and supportive experience on your website. We will focus on marketing your site, site organization, and security ideas to develop your buying process.

## Describing the elements of the online web transaction

Every online transaction has three core components: The transaction page, the merchant account, and the payment gateway. Let's look at these 3 in detail.

- **The transaction page-** This is where the buyer enters their contact and credit card information that is usually built into a formal shopping cart program that accepts different payment types. There are fields to enter their billing information, shipping, and tax information as well.

- **Shopping Cart –** The absolute most common and well-known way to sell products and services online is through the internet-based ordering system known as a shopping cart. A visitor places an order on your site and clicks the add button to load the product or service into the shopping cart. When you're using a shopping cart and its set it up correctly, you can be making orders immediately as long as you have the other components setup as well, the merchant account and the gateway.

- **Merchant Account-** You must have a merchant account company that agreed to accept credit card information for online transactions. This account allows you to track credit card transactions on the internet. One of the most popular accounts you will see is a **PayPal account.**

- **Go to www.paypal.com for more details, PayPal is a great way to get started, and it's very simple to setup.**

There are many merchant accounts services online to choose from; contact anyone that will be a great fit for your own business needs, Google them.

## The payment gateways

A **payment gateway** is a merchant service provided by an e-commerce application service provider that authorizes credit card or direct payments processing for e-businesses, online retailers, or traditional brick and mortar businesses.

## The shopping cart setup for business success

Please understand, it's very important to successfully setup your shopping cart to sell your products and services online.

1. Make sure your shopping cart displays the item description, the quantity being ordered, and the ordering page's price.
2. Ensure you have clearly displayed the PayPal or credit card information or both that can be used as a payment source.
3. Make sure you remove all navigation buttons from the order page not to make it easy for the buyer to exit the purchasing process.
4. Create a custom thank you page for each product sold.
5. Create an auto responder for each product that emails the customer upon purchase.

Check out: http://www.cloudnet360.com/how-it-works/shoppingcart.html

Cloudnet360- is an excellent solution for all levels of web marketers and businesses.

- Easy to setup and use
- Free technical support
- Lots of amazing features to use
- Custom thank you pages and much more…

Here are some important things to think about if you have a product or service that people want to buy from you. You must make sure your product or service is the answer to their problem or pain point. Remember, your job is to provide the information or solution to your customers' needs, at the same time, provide an easy ordering or buying process for them.

- How long will it take to get their order?
- Is their data and contact information secured?
- Is this a legitimate company or business operation?
- Who do they contact if they have a problem?

- Where do they go for a refund if needed?
- How soon will their credit card be charged?
- Are they ordering the correct product?
- Are they getting the best value for their dollar?

Make sure you answer the questions above, either in your sales copy or during the ordering process, to make your customers feel secure and confident they are getting the best value for their money.

## Here are some ways to increase your new customer revenue

One critical thing to secure your business success is you must offer an excellent product and or service to every customer. If you do this, you will have no problem getting them to purchase other items from your business. You should list all the products you could promote, and you will be on your way to maximizing every potential customer sale.

Every successful business has multiple products or services for sale at different price ranges that allow them the possibility to up-sell, cross-sell, and back end sales. Let's look at these in further detail.

## Up-selling

Up-selling is just a way of persuading someone or a customer to buy a more expensive product of what they already decided to buy. An example would be when someone is buying a book from you for $25, and when they get to the order page, they are made a special offer to purchase a DVD set of the book instead of $75.

## Cross-selling

This is just promoting additional accessories to a standard product during the payment process of a transaction. Let's say that someone buys a book from you for $25. During the final transaction, you feature a special offer that the customer can add, a complimentary DVD to the purchase; this is cross-selling.

When trying to cross-sell, always make sure you have confirmed the initial sale first and then offer the additional product option after the original purchase is completed.

## Back-end selling

Back-end selling promotes products on the back-end of a purchase transaction the customer has taken an interest in. If your customer bought a book from you, then you could offer a workbook, audio files, online course, or videos as complements to the book. Each of your offers should be a compliment or enhance the value of the product they just purchased.

## Producing more web traffic for your business

The ability to generate web traffic to your site requires spending plenty of time drawing in and attracting visitors. You can do this either by paying a service to draw them to you directly or hiring a sales team to do the work for you. Let's look at some ways to generate traffic to your website now.

- **Advertise-** Paid search and display advertising are all excellent ways of attracting visitors and building your brand, and getting your site in front of people. Adjust your paid strategies to suit your goals.
- **Going social-** One of the best ways to increase traffic to your website is to use social media to promote your content. You know, like: Twitter, Google, YouTube, and LinkedIn.
- **Write great headlines-** Headlines are one of the most important parts of your content writing. Without an amazing headline, even the most detailed websites will go unnoticed. Master the art of amazing headline writing.

- **SEO optimization-** Optimizing your content for search engines is a super valuable and an important practice you should learn how to do. Are you creating internal links to new content on your site? What about meta-tag descriptions? Learn all you can about them.
- **Blogging-** Blogging can increase blog traffic to your website and help build your brand into the amazing product or service that it is. Be careful; the blogging standards have changed during the past couple of years, so learn how to blog properly so you don't get into trouble.
- Go to: http://www.theblogbuilders.com/how-to-start-a-blog
- **Writing and posting to LinkedIn-** LinkedIn has become much more than a means of finding another job. The world's largest professional social network is now a valuable publishing platform, which means you should regularly post content to LinkedIn.
- **Interviewing industry leaders-** Send out emails requesting an interview with your industries top leaders and publish the interviews on your blog. Not only will the name recognition boost your credibility and increase traffic to your website, but you could make a name for yourself and your business.

These are just a few ways to generate traffic to your website. If you're hoping to get more traffic to your site that will result in more sales, you'll need to target as many different niche' markets as you can as a part of your web traffic strategies. It can take a lot of work and be expensive, but the payoff can be worth it in profits.

## How to create your own affiliate program to gain profits

Start by trying to imagine the benefits and the profits you can make by having other people or businesses promoting your products or service to a large audience. Let's learn how to create your own affiliate program so others can help you become successful and profitable.

**The steps to affiliate success**

1.  **Create a great product-** The first thing you need is a great product that people will love. It would be best if you had something worth becoming excited about in the mind of an advertiser or marketer, and this is what you will be asking of your affiliates exactly. Develop your product until you have full confidence in it for the market that you serve.

2.  **Choose the right affiliate platform-** You must get connected to the most popular affiliate platforms that exist today. This is where affiliates can add an account for themselves and get links to promote your product or services.

3.  **Recruit affiliates to represent your products and your brand-** Connect with marketers that you can search out and invite to promote your products or services. Make sure they can hit the ground running! Making you money is one of the huge advantages of working with a great affiliate company.

## How to attract affiliates to your products

After your affiliate program is setup, announce to your customers that you're looking for people to recommend your products and services to others, and you pay referral fees. Some of the best and easiest people to help you promote are those people who have used your products and services in the past. Send an email or some other communication form to your clients to announce your amazing products from your affiliate program.

Depending on what you're selling in your affiliate program and its price, determines how many affiliates you will need for your success. The more affiliates you have, the higher the potential profits to be made, so try to get as many as you can. One of the important things you want to do is provide your affiliates with all of your best promotions and sales copy in their efforts to promote your products or services.

## The Joint Venture- How it can increase your sales

A joint venture is when you partner with another business or experts to sell your products or services to their customers. They provide the customers, and you provide the products, services, or expertise. This is a joint venture. Most successful joint ventures want to sell your products or services in huge quantities and make equally huge profits for what and who they bring to the table.

**Here are some steps to success in a joint venture**

- Look for strong partners – Businesses with important skills or resources you can benefit from.
- Make sure that your contribution to the deal is equal to your partner's.
- Make your agreements simple but put them in writing for legal reasons.
- Establish clear rules at the beginning for amending or dissolving the relationship if it fails to meet both of your expectations.
- You want your partner to benefit from the relationship as much as you do.

## How to make a connection with a joint venture partner

**Here are some steps you can take to find a joint venture partner**

- **Go to events where you can network with potential partners-** You have to put yourself and your business in the face of people looking for a joint venture opportunity. These people can help you take your business to the next level. Explain to them in a presentation the upside and value of partnering with you and your business, and you may need to show them the numbers.

- **Referrals** - Your customers and associates may likely know someone who could be a possible joint venture partner for your business. The idea is to persuade the right partner to do business with you. Present your case to them to make things happen.

- **Some things to present to the potential partner-** You may want to present your potential partner with a sales volume report, a website customer visitation report, or even some testimonials from happy customers to get their attention.

- **Helping your partner understand your product value-** Help your partner understand how his followers can benefit from your product or service. Assure the partner that you genuinely care about the customer and the people who use the product or service you are providing them with.

In closing, we have covered quite a bit of important information on making money with your internet business. You should try to evaluate everything you have learned and see if you can apply it to your own business model for your online business success. Not everything will work for every business, but the information we have provided you with is very popular amongst many successful online businesses that exist in the market today.

# CHAPTER 28

# THE BEST WEBSITE DESIGN THAT WILL BRING YOU SUCCESS

**What you will learn in this chapter**

- ➢ The purpose of a superior website design
- ➢ How to make sure there are no hold-ups to your sales success
- ➢ Utilizing a branding process for your Success
- ➢ The legal process and what you need to understand
- ➢ Measuring your site for its effectiveness

For the success of your business on the internet, you must have a superior and amazing website that must also provide amazing products and services that you will sell to your customers. You must have a website design that your customers will love.

This chapter is dedicated to helping you understand website design techniques that will help your customers navigate your site with ease and comfort. You will learn about company branding, using the right colors, and the right graphics to draw in their attention. You will get a good understanding about the important areas of the web page layout and the proper ways to design a site that is easy to use.

## Understanding the branding process

Branding is the marketing practice of creating a name or a design that identifies and differentiates your product or service from other products and services on the market. An effective branding strategy will give you an edge over the competition in a competitive market.

**Understanding the importance of a tagline and the slogan-** The tagline or slogan is a short phrase that communicates to your customers about who you are and what you or your products represent.

## Your company logo and why it is so important

Your logo is a visual icon of your company's brand. Your company identity is visually expressed through its logo, which, along with your company name, is one of the main things that will make your business memorable. It's super important to have an amazing company or product logo. A good logo will help you tremendously, and it clarifies who you are and what you're all about to your customers. It will help them understand important information about your product and services for all visitors to your site immediately. The logo helps remind people of your company and what you do without even seeing the products you make. Visitors will be able to associate your business based on your company logo that was developed to represent you.

**Some logo software and sites to get one created for your business.**

- https://www.canva.com
- www.fiverr.com
- https://www.logomaker.com
- https://www.tailorbrands.com

## List of Best Logo Design Software for designers

1. Adobe Illustrator
2. CorelDraw
3. Adobe Photoshop
4. GIMP
5. Inkscape
6. Canva
7. Hatchful by Shopify
8. Affinity Designer
9. Gravit Designer
10. Adobe Spark

## How to make sure your web text styling is correct

One of the very crucial and important elements you need to think about and consider on your website is how and what type of font size and font type you're using. You want to experiment with different fonts to see which one works best for your website and the message you're trying to push.

**What colors should I use on my website?** Please understand that using the right colors on your website is very important and could mean the difference between a visitor buying from you or not. The colors you use should be one of the most important decisions you make with your website design.

## Understanding the colors and what they mean in business

Go to this interesting site for more information: http://www.empower-yoursel f-with-color-psychology.com/website-colors.html

Color has a powerful effect on our lives, in everything that we do and see without ever saying a word. Having a basic understanding of color meaning in the business world gives us the ability to get the best response in our marketing and promotional efforts and ultimately create a successful business.

## The importance of high-quality photos for your site

Have you ever thought about what your photos on your site are saying to your visitors? We live in a visual age where images, photos, and clipart are surrounding us. Whether on your website, marketing materials, billboards, or ads, the photos you choose to represent your products and services are very important.

- Use exciting photos to represent your products or services.
- Do not photograph your products on a busy shelf. Rather, show them in use in an appropriate environment.
- Hire a professional photographer to shoot and edit your product and web photos if needed.

**You can also buy photos from an online gallery or stock photo company; check out the following:**

- https://www.shutterstock.com
- www.pixabay.com
- www.unslash.com
- http://www.istockphoto.com
- www.bigstockphoto.com

There are many more online vendors to choose from.

## Proper layout of your web page content

One of the best and easiest ways to get a cool or amazing website layout is to use a template. You can check out some of these website companies for your web template.

- http://www.opendesigns.org
- https://www.squarespace.com
- www.godaddy.com
- www.wix.com
- https://www.freewebtemplates.com
- https://www.templatemonster.com/free-templates.php#gref

There are many more vendors to choose from on the internet.

Every page on any website should feature plenty of opportunities for visitors to take some type of action.

- Buying your products or services.
- Requesting more information regarding some item you sell.
- Signing up for a newsletter or a report of some kind.
- Connecting with you socially, such as Face book, Twitter, etc.

Remember, your website is a virtual online store, and you need to setup your store so when the visitor enters it, he or she can get the right to the product, service, or information that they are looking for right away. The first thing you want them to notice is your amazing product headline in the center of the page. Let's take a look at an amazing layout that grabs attention. https://xtremeteez.com

Many site layouts use the upper right quadrant area for the **about us section** that usually has data on when the company started and contact information, on many websites, you may also see.

- Special promotions your company may offer.
- Important company news or updates.
- A search box or navigation box.
- Contact information.

## The importance of the horizontal navigation bar

The horizontal navigation bar is the area you see going across the top of the web page. This bar's main purpose is to get your visitors to navigate around your site to get to all of your other pages within your website. Take a look at the www.amazon.com site to see a great layout.

Once a visitor comes to your site, most are there because you have a product or service they need or want. When setting up your company navigation bar, you will need to decide what important information or features are most important to your visitors and then set these up on your navigation bar to make it easy for your visitors to get what they want or need immediately. Let's look at some common navigation bar setups.

- **Home page-** Make sure your visitors can get back to your home page fast if needed.
- **Our products or services-** Make it easy for your visitors to get to one of the most important areas of your webpage.
- **About or contact us page-** Make it easy for the visitor to get hold or contact you with questions if they have them.
- **Testimonials or blogs-** If you want to earn a visitor's trust and credibility, you will want these on the navigation bar.

The most important thing to remember in the navigation bar is that it's designed to get the visitor to take some action. Use the navigation bar to get people interested in your website and get them to review and look for more information.

**Let's now look at when and how to decide on using buttons, arrows, hyperlinks, scrolling, and clicking on features.**

- A **button** simply is used to get the visitor to do something on a website. If there is a field to input something for data, then you want to use a button.

- Using **the arrow** is very important when you're instructing the user on what you need them to do on your site. The arrow is a guide to the user to lead them somewhere on your website.
- **Hyper-Links** are primarily used for links to other pages where visitors can get more specific content on an important subject. They are generally underlined and colored in a blue appearance.
- **Scrolling vs. clicking** Many different websites use scrolling and clicking features to help visitors navigate their sites. Generally speaking, when you have clicked on a specific link from a webpage of interest, people don't mind scrolling through the information if it provides them with what they are looking for. The information absolutely must be valuable and peak interest to make people want to scroll down and read more.

## Creating and designing your optimal website

When it's time to begin the creation and the design of your website, here is what you should do first. The first thing you absolutely must do is create a website design plan, which includes collecting important information for your layout.

- What is the primary goal of your website?
- Create a written description of your business, company info, business slogan, logo design, and location information.
- Research and list several websites that you love and build your layout accordingly.
- Decide on what navigation buttons and information you want on the site
- Figure out how many products or services you will sell and what type of shopping cart you will need.
- Once the site is built, are all links functional and easy for the visitor to navigate?

Before you complete your website launch, you should always have your website tested by multiple people you trust and in all types of browsers to make sure it is completely functioning the way you want it to. Remember, your website will begin to promote your business products and services to the entire world, so your layout and design are critical to your success.

## Creating and launching multiple websites to expand your web presence

Remember, your core business website is your online face to the world and should be developed and created with this in mind. Now, let's look at some supplemental websites you can use to drive even more traffic to your main website. Adding these additional websites to your main site can help you become an even more important business in your industry and position you to dominate the competition. Remember, whenever you're building different and supportive websites, you must have an amazing design and excellent web content to grab the visitor's attention.

We promote using the word press method as a great choice for building websites. To learn a little bit more about Word Press, go to www.wordpress.com

- It's super easy to customize and very easy to learn.
- It works great with Google search engines.
- It is very easy to view on mobile devices. You just need the right plugins.
- There is tons of support due to its popularity in the market today.

## Steps to setup a word press website for your business

1. First, go and register your company domain name.
   - • http://www.domain.com
   - • Or go to https://www.godaddy.com

2. Start by getting your website hosting account setup, there are many to choose from, but we like https://www.godaddy.com. They support word press with no problems at all.

3. Setup your preferences, plugins, and shopping cart software as needed.

4. Setup your website design, whether you use a theme or a custom design.

5. Add all of your business pages in the theme or custom design accordingly.

After you have your core website setup, you can automatically deliver important content to the entire world using this cool and exciting tool called **Deliver It** to have smart social media automation. This is the best way to find and share great content on Face book, Twitter, Pinterest, and more.

- https://dlvrit.com

There are free and paid accounts you can set with **Deliver it.** Go to the website, setup your account, and follow the simple, easy steps to instant smart social media automation. When you publish your blogs or content, it is automatically sent to the proper networks you choose to connect using the program.

There are alternatives to **Deliver it**- https://dlvrit.com that exist as well.

- https://hootsuite.com
- https://www.zoho.com/social
- https://sproutsocial.com
- https://www.agorapulse.com
- https://www.sendible.com

## Driving traffic to supplement your core website

Let's now look at two excellent additions to your overall web marketing strategies that we feel are great choices and can bring more visitors and revenue to your online business.

- www.wordpress.com
- www.wix.com
- www.hostgator.com
- https://www.networksolutions.com
- www.site123.com
- https://www.squarespace.com
- www.weebly.com

And https://www.blogger.com

- **All of these sources can draw more traffic to your site-** All you have to do is regularly add great content to either account, and you have the potential possibility to gain more followers and getting more traffic to your site.
- **Use these sources to add company links-** All you need to do when you're blogging about a particular subject is just put links in the blog that lead back to your main site.
- **Getting larger search engine shares-** You can use the two mediums to create blog content that allows you to get more search space on the engine by linking your search results back to your main site.

## How to generate web traffic with content accumulator sites

This refers to a web site or computer software program that accumulates a specific type of information from multiple online sources. Your content site can bring a large variety of people searching for specific or multiple topics related to your business industry. You will collect information on goods and services from several competing sources on this website.

## Top 4 content aggregator websites

1. **https://alltop.com** - All top is the best content aggregator website; it has an Alexa rank of 6,800.

2. **http://www.blogengage.com** - Blog engagement is an excellent way of getting your content seen by many people.

3. **www.bizsugar.com** – Biz Sugar is another content website that allows you to submit news, specifically news related to small businesses.

4. **http://www.blokube.com** -BloKube is great for getting exposure to your blog and network with other bloggers, which is good for building relationships with other bloggers of similar niches.

## What about setting up a paid membership website

A membership website simply allows visitors to get a username and or password to get access to content on a secure site. Setting up a membership website is not that hard to do. You have to decide what type of content and features you want the visitors to access. No matter what road you decide to take, you will need to attach your shopping cart or payment processing system to the site to get your payments from the members every month.

One of the most important things to do to get members to sign up on your membership website is to create a special program for members only. This has to be valuable to the members that they will be willing to keep paying a monthly fee for years to come.

**Here are a couple of things you should do before you launch your membership website.**

- **Monthly fees-** How much are you going to charge your members to access the site?
- **Participation-** You will need to know at what level you want to be engaged in the daily or monthly updates needed to supply your members with great content or products.

Membership websites can bring in a high monthly income to you and your business if you set it up right and give your members a product or service of high value that they would be willing to pay for.

In closing, if you want to increase visitor traffic and make money online with your website, you must try to follow the steps that we have laid out here for you. Your website design, content, and products and services must be amazing to capture your visitors' attention and get them to spend money with you. If you follow the steps we have discussed, you should see a higher level of success in your business than not doing anything at all.

# CHAPTER 29

# HOW TO PRODUCE AMAZING
## WEB CONTENT THAT PROMOTES YOUR BUSINESS

**What you will learn in this chapter**

- ➤ How to write powerful and captivating web content
- ➤ The fundamentals of using landing, squeeze, and sales pages
- ➤ How to encourage and inspire your customers to purchase your products or services

There are plenty of websites that exist today that have a hard time converting their visitors into buyers of their products and services, and this is because the content on their page does not excite the visitors to purchase from them. Several studies have shown that you must have great and exciting web content that inspires visitors to purchase your products and or services that add value into their lives.

When trying to write content for your website, always use proven methods that have worked forever. As a creator of a business on the internet, it's your role to develop content that will compel the visitors into believing they are in the right place and that you have the right product or service from the right company.

# Learn the most important elements of amazing web content

1. **Treat your visitors like they are the most important people ever-** Remember, your visitors are searching for information or a product to buy that fills a need, so you must make them feel like they absolutely must have your product or services or your special offer.

2. **Make it easy for your visitors to find you-** Whatever the visitor is looking for, you need to make it very easy to find your products or services online; the easier it is the better for your business.

3. **Put your most important information first-** The most important information to your web visitors is often a simple statement of what you do or a catchy headline about your products or service. Once they understand what you do, they might want to know some more important details about the product or services that you offer.

4. **Be very honest and be creative-** Speak honestly about your products and services to the visitor and be creative in the sense of helping them understand the value that the product or service might bring into their lives.

5. **Write for people with short attention spans-** Web visitors don't want to make a huge effort to read your text, so make your copy easy to read.
   - Use short paragraphs – four sentences max
   - Use short sentences – twelve words on average
   - Address your visitors directly
   - Avoid using jargon or long-winded words

## The importance of an amazing headline

Remember, you only have a few seconds to grab the visitor's attention and keep it when it comes to web traffic. So, your headline must be very eye-catching and effective. The headline has one core purpose: to grab the reader's attention and intrigue them into reading or wanting more information. Let's look at some catchy and cool headlines.

- THE SECRET OF MAKING PEOPLE LIKE YOU......
- WHY SOME PEOPLE ALMOST ALWAYS MAKE MONEY IN THE STOCKMARKET
- HOW I IMPROVED MY MEMORY IN ONE EVENING?
- DISCOVER THE FORTUNE THAT LIES HIDDEN IN YOUR SALARY
- HOW TO WIN FRIENDS AND INFLUENCE PEOPLE
- YOU CAN LAUGH AT MONEY WORRIES - IF YOU FOLLOW THIS SIMPLE PLAN
- RIGHT AND WRONG FARMING METHODS - AND LITTLE POINTERS THAT WILL INCREASE YOUR PROFITS
- NEW CAKE IMPROVER GETS YOU COMPLIMENTS LIKE CRAZY!
- THOUSANDS OF PEOPLE NOW PLAY WHO NEVER THOUGHT THEY COULD
- GREAT NEW DISCOVERY KILLS KITCHEN ODORS QUICKLY!

These are just a few cool and catchy headlines that have made people tons of money that have used them or something similar. Once you have written your headline for your business, you need to make sure it is centered on the page, has the right color to bring out the excitement about the product or information, and has the correct font size to bring attention to the words immediately.

## Important tips for the body of the message

In the body of the message, you must demonstrate that you have the answer or solution to the problem the visitor is looking for.

- With millions of choices at their fingertips, internet users prefer to scan content quickly to find results. If they don't find what they are looking for, they will quickly leave your site and go with your competition.

- Make your content valuable and relevant to your customers. Make sure you are providing information that is relevant to their search. Otherwise, they are gone in a matter of seconds.
- Keep your content brief and stay on topic. Visitors can become frustrated if they are forced to sort through a lot of information to find what they are looking for. If you have very broad topics, consider breaking your content down and introducing one topic per paragraph so your readers can find specific information easily.
- Try making your content readable and engaging for the people visiting your site. Your goal is to convert visitors into customers. Use a conversational manner to connect with your audience.

Creating content for your business website can be a challenge, but you can be sure that your copy is valuable and engaging to your readers by following these simple tips.

## Getting your customer to take action and purchase something

Always make it easy to take the next step, which is buying something of value from you.

- Make sure your contact information and phone numbers are readily available.
- Remember to keep all of your <u>text links underlined</u> and in blue color.
- Make sure the exit process leads the visitors to your ordering page; don't allow them to get distracted by too much information you want them to have an easy and fun ordering experience.
- Make sure your high probability customers have a continuous stream of value until they're ready to buy your products or services.

- Various technology tools make it easy to automate the closing process like up-selling or cross-selling.
- You've already built a solid relationship with your customers based on value and trust, so now it makes you the logical choice when it comes time for them to make another buying decision.

## The fundamentals of the landing, squeeze, and sales pages

A **"Landing Page"** is any page on the website which someone might land on that has a form and exists mainly to capture a visitor's information through that form. Whatever method the visitor uses to find you on the internet, the first page on your website that people will see is known as your Landing Page. Your landing page has to be perfect and have the product or solution the visitor is looking for. Remember, the landing page must have a form and must exist solely to capture a visitor's information through that form.

Example: A form on a landing page is an opportunity for someone to convert. That conversion event could be filling out a form for an e-book, filling out their email address so they can subscribe to your blog, or filling out transactional information to purchase a product on your site.

- First name
- Last name
- Email address
- Phone number

With your landing pages, you want them to be content-specific or subject-specific on your website and drive traffic to those pages to expose the visitors to all of your products and services and or possible solutions you can provide for them.

## The squeeze page - and how they work

A Squeeze Page is a landing page designed to capture opt-in email addresses from potential subscribers. A squeeze page's goal is to convince, persuade, or otherwise **"squeeze"** a visitor into providing one of their most important pieces of personal data, their email address.

The secret here is to gather as much targeted traffic as possible for your specific product, the topic of interest, or blogging communication. You will want to inspire these visitors to sign up or be a part of your mailing list so you can introduce them to products or ideas that interest them in which you may have some level of skill or expertise.

- First name
- Last name
- Email address

Here are some added things you will need to have a successful squeeze page for your business.

- They must have an amazing and catchy headline for starters.
- Generally, have a high-quality photo for the person seeking the information.
- It must be written in a personable manner for visitor comfort.
- Should have bullet points with all the benefits or value on the subject at hand.
- You should always have something of value that you're willing to give away to the visitor as a good-faith measure. The visitors need to trust you with their important email information.
- As a rule of thumb, most squeeze pages usually have two fields, but no more than four. Keep it as simple as possible.
- Remember, the visitor agrees to give you his or her email address and, in return, are expecting you to give them what they came for. Make sure you honor this agreement.

## The sales and informative content pages- How they work

The sale page, also known as click-through landing pages, nurtures your visitors directly on your site and is a more advanced marketing technique. They are sort of a combination of lead generation and direct sales landing pages. Their purpose is to warm leads through a sales funnel directly on your site.

- These pages teach and educate the visitor about the core facts on a particular product, service, or topic of interest.
- They help coach and inform the visitor with enough information so they can make an intelligent decision.
- The information you put on a sales page should be enough for a person to make a knowledgeable decision.
- They are ultimately designed to convert the visitor into a paying customer.

## Informative and educational content pages- How they work

Informative and educational content pages are generally used to educate people about specific problems or issues they are faced with. An educational landing page is a standalone web page designed to get visitors to take the desired action. The action can range from the request for more detailed information to inform them how some applications or processes can enhance their lives.

- Usually, they are short in nature and very fast to create.
- Keep the user-focused because they are generally based on a specific subject or topic.
- They are built using specific keywords that make them easy to find for the viewer.

- Allow you to educate or suggest a solution to the specific problem or subject at hand.
- You have the opportunity to gain the interest of many visitors in a short time span.

**How to create a follow up using informative or educational pages**

1. One of the best ways to begin is to check out hot topics that concern many people or check out the latest forums to see what people are talking about right now. You will want to make sure when you begin to have a catchy headline to start with.

2. You will want to start with either a solution to a problem people are having or help them figure out a problem they are dealing with in life.

3. Help the visitor understand how they can get through the issue with some easy steps to use and try using some bullet points here.

4. You will want to talk about an outline that summarizes overall solutions and how you can assist or help with the problems they are faced with.

5. Make sure there is a section that identifies who you are and your credentials.

6. Make sure you have links on the page that link the user to your main page or website to get even more information on the subject.

# How to inspire your visitors to purchase your products or services

Getting traffic to your website is clearly what we all want to happen, but if that traffic doesn't convert into paying customers, it's almost useless. This section will outline some strategies for getting your visitors to take action, whether that's filling out a form, handing over their email address, or making a purchase.

When the visitor comes to your site, what is the first thing they will see? That would be your captivating headline; make sure, whenever possible, your headline is based on what people are looking for and what they want the most.

## Some simple steps for success

1. You must clearly state the benefits of your product or service. Let your visitors know exactly what you can do for them or what problem you will solve for them right up front.

2. Get your visitors excited. Use emotionally-stimulating language and amazing information to get your visitors ready and excited to try your product or services.

3. Include consumer reviews. There is no doubt that consumer reviews are extremely important in helping people make purchase decisions.

4. Offer various payment options. Consider offering a variety of payment methods to satisfy the preferences of all your potential customers.

5. Add a guarantee. Include a refund policy on all purchases. This reduces risk, and the increased sales you get will make up for any returns that may come.

In closing, we have given you the full details on what you must do regarding web content, landing pages, squeeze pages, and sales content pages. If you follow the details we have discussed, you can expect an increase in visitor traffic and sales conversion. Spend some valuable time working on the super important web content for your business, and once you get that completed, you will see the potential sales from your focused efforts.

# CHAPTER 30

# BUILDING YOUR BUSINESS WITH POTENTIAL PROSPECTS & WHEN TO HIRE AN INTERNET OR WEB SERVICE PROVIDER

**What you will learn in this chapter**

- ➢ Developing exciting ways individuals can reach you on the web
- ➢ How to connect with visitors when they come to visit your site
- ➢ How to use social media to grow your sales and your business
- ➢ Getting the help, you need with your internet and marketing goals

When you finally have your website up and operational, it's important to understand that the main reason you even have a business on the internet is to build up a following and make money with that following by selling your products and services to them.

This chapter is designed to educate you on how to bring in targeted traffic to your website and to turn that traffic into potential purchasing prospects.

## Setting up the right contact forms

When you design or create a contact form, you are guiding the visitors on your website and getting them to do something. The correct forms on your website are a very important tool that allows you to make contact, sign up customers for a newsletter, or even get your visitor to give you some important information you may need from them in the future.

The simplest of web forms contain no more than three fields: *Name, Email, and Message,* but of course, you can tweak or adjust them as needed. Below are the five common form types:

1. The contact form
2. The lead generation form
3. The order form
4. Event registration form
5. The survey form

**Seven best practices for web forms**

1. **The number of fields should not exceed six, for most cases.**
2. **Match the color scheme of your form with your brand.**
3. **Use checkboxes, radio buttons, etc. Place instructions where confusion may occur.**
4. **Make fields appear only upon user input.**
5. **Do not ask for private information like phone number, email address unless needed. Where more sensitive information is requested, link to your privacy policy.**
6. **For longer forms, divide content into sections.**
7. **Publish forms in the spots where they are properly visible.**

If you need easy ready-made forms that can be customized for your business, visit the form companies below.

- www.perfectforms.com
- www.formsite.com
- www.formstack.com
- https://www.jotform.com
- https://www.cognitoforms.com
- https://www.fastfieldforms.com/index.html

## The amazing potential of online chat services

Phone support is the traditional method of supporting your customers for many big companies, but it can be very costly. Live chat doesn't cost much more than a quality email provider. Live chat enables your team members to assist several visitors at once. Let's look at some of the benefits of live chat services.

- It's convenient for your customers
- Cuts down on business expenses
- Increases sales and builds trust with your customers
- Gives you an edge over the competition

When people want support, they generally want it immediately. Live chat is one of those amazing services that answer this problem for your visitors or guest. Let's look at some live chat service providers now.

1. https://www.ruby.com
2. https://acquire.io
3. https://www.zendesk.com
4. www.chatoutsource.com
5. https://www.supportninja.com
6. www.processflows.co.uk

Next, here is a list of the top live chat software products for 2019

- Live Chat
- Fresh Desk
- ZohoSales IQ
- Live Agent
- Desk.com
- Olark
- Happy Fox Chat
- Chat Blazer
- Zen desk Chat
- Cingo
- What desk

## Using social media to build website traffic

It's now very common to use social media when a visitor comes to your site to shop around or even make a purchase. They also will want to know what social media platforms you and your businesses are connected to. Many visitors will stay connected and monitor what you and your business are up to in the world of social media. Every web-based business absolutely must engage in social media these days, and they will want to post a blog and tweet about the important topic of the day to stay relevant and build up a following.

**Twitter-** Use Twitter daily to tweet about things that are of interest to you or interest to your followers. You want to create communication with your followers regularly.

**Face book-** Face book is one of the most popular ways to make personal connections with visitors or guests to your website. Always steer the communication to lead the visitor back to your website in a casual way.

**YouTube-** If you have great videos of your products or any new informational products, you will want to create a YouTube channel. You want to upload your amazing or hot product or service videos here. Educational videos are a very popular type of video that visitors love to watch on YouTube.

**LinkedIn-** With LinkedIn, you definitely want to join a popular niche' group and offer your expert advice on a particular subject that may be up for discussion. There are many working professionals on LinkedIn, so you will want to brush up and be very polished here.

**Pinterest and Snap Chat are social media platforms that have mainly artists** and young people using them with their artist friends. You can also use Snap Chat to launch new products. Or you can use Pinterest as well.

**Here are some tips and strategic ways to use Pinterest for marketing**

- Create boards with keywords in your title.
- Use the description to spread your ideas.
- Create vertical images to maximize your real estate.
- Build relevant links back to your website or blog.
- Embed pins on your blog.

Your customers and visitors are interacting with many different businesses and friends through social media. So, having a strong **social media marketing plan** in place on the web is the key to tapping into their interest and getting your products and services into their faces. If done properly, **marketing with social media can bring incredible success to your business.**

## Getting the help you need with your internet business and goals

When starting your internet business, you can start with a small amount of money and grow your company as large as you want. You will need to plan for your business very well and monitor every aspect of your company's budget and overhead spending. One of the biggest decisions you will need to make in setting up your business is choosing what part of the process you want to accomplish on your own and what task you want to pay a vendor or web service provider to accomplish for you.

In this section, you will learn and understand how to build a team of people who can help you build and maintain your web business. If the setup process becomes overwhelming, you can then choose to hire a vendor or web service provider to build, support, and maintain your entire online business for you.

## Building an internet marketing team

To boost internet and web traffic for your business, you have some core positions you will need to fill. All of these positions will help you get your business off the ground and get you up and running quickly.

- **The marketing expert-** Helps your business by designing your brand, logos, and slogans. They will also help you with promotions and packaging if you need it.
- **Website Designer-** This is part of the website design process. They can create a website that looks great on any device that your customers will love.
- **Internet marketing expert-** They assess what the competition is doing. They can create web content and strategies to maximize your profit and sales potential.
- **Social media expert-** They can set up accounts for all social media platforms and design strategies for Google, Face book, LinkedIn, and Twitter. They can monitor your content and receive requests from followers on your social media platforms.

Building the right team to support your business takes some serious thought and planning on your part. You will need to consider all the skills needed for your business to succeed. You will need to understand which skill-sets you already have and which positions you will need to outsource to a vendor or web service provider.

## How to choose the right vendor or web service provider

There are many things you can do by yourself to setup and maintain your internet business. For many of the long hour task, you will need to consider building a team of well-established professionals that have an excellent business track record. With the right team in place, you can effectively increase profits and build your visitor and customer base in a short amount of time.

**The Vendors** and **Web Service Providers** are companies or individuals with various skills and services that you can benefit from. You need to know what skills and services you're willing to pay for and get the right person to get the job done. Who you choose to work with largely depends on your financial budget and the working relationship you both have agreed upon.

Some of the best vendors and web service providers are popular companies with a huge team of highly trained individuals who can work under pressure and meet critical deadlines promptly. Below is a list of some very popular web service providers with a well known and proven background and track record.

- **Fiverr-** www.fiverr.com - Find services based on your goals and deadlines; it's that simple.
- **Up Work-** https://www.upwork.com – In-demand talent that is on demand.
- **Toptal-** https://www.toptal.com – Best talent on the market at great prices.
- **SEO Clerks-** www.seoclerk.com – They have thousands of SEO experts and services that start at $1.
- **Five Squid-** www.fivesquid.com – Located in the UK, you'll be amazed at what people can do for £5, £10, £20, or £50. You can also create custom orders and post requests.

- **Guru** - www.guru.com - Find & Hire Talented Freelancers.
- **Gig bucks**- www.gigbucks.com - Hire expert digital marketers, creators& more from $5 to $50.
- **99designs**- www.99designs.com - Find and work with talented freelance designers online 364,571 happy customers. A design you love or your money back.
- **Craigslist**- www.craigslist.com - Local classifieds and forums - community moderated, and largely free.

There are many other web service providers to choose from. You just need to assess your business needs and then do a little research on Google to find exactly what you're looking for.

## How to ask for referrals and get more resources for the business

Referrals are one of the top ways to not only grow your business, but find good help for your web marketing strategies and projects you may need help with now and into the future. What you may not have realized is that you can exponentially increase the number of referrals you can get and dramatically increase your business opportunities by doing one simple thing - **asking for referrals.** Having the right referral can help you grow your business and get you more of the results you're looking for.

## Discovering the right vendor, web service provider, or referral for the Job

Once you have decided on a particular **Web Service Provider**, you can follow these steps to confirm if they are right for you.

1.  Start with having a list of questions you want to be answered, such as *"how long have you been in business?"*

2. You will want to know how they will charge you—charging by the hour, weekly, or by the project completion.

3. Do they have experience working with businesses like yours? Are they knowledgeable about the issues and technologies relevant to your organization?

4. Can they respond quickly to evolving market conditions?

5. Do they offer proactive monitoring and reporting services that can alert you to potential failures?

6. Are they flexible and scalable enough to serve both short-term peaks and long-term business needs?

Remember, when you ask for a referral, be sincere and direct. Remind yourself that the worst that can happen is that the client says, **"No."**

## Should I outsource my projects and when to do it?

Many businesses form partnerships with suppliers as well as with contractors. Working with outside contractors or outsourcing can allow companies to do business more professionally and effectively. Companies generally outsource in one of two ways they outsource a single component of their daily operations or establish outsourcing as a strategic part of their business. Here are some things you will want to clarify in your communication and dealing with an outsourced vendor.

- Communication frequency is critical to performance and operations, so decide with the vendor on what time and when you need to meet and talk about the project you both have agreed to.
- Keep in mind that outsourcing requires you to establish goals and a timeline with your contractors.
- You have to be aware of differences in culture and language. For example, contractors may not be aware of the "language" you use within your own company.
- One-time events also work hand-in-hand with outsourcing.

When properly handled, outsourcing can enable you to simplify your business operations. It can help you to maneuver your resources more strategically, maximize your time, and move forward with important growth initiatives now.

In closing, we have discussed in detail the many different components of hiring contractors, web service providers, and marketing specialists. You now must decide which option is the right one for you and your business. You must also decide which services you would like to outsource to a vendor that you may not be so great at. Whatever you decide to do, just make sure you are in full agreement with the vendor to accomplish your desired goals.

# CHAPTER 31

# SEARCH ENGINE OPTIMIZATION (SEO) & WEB ANALYTICS SUCCESS

**What you will learn in this chapter**

- ➢ Understanding the search engine & the ranking system
- ➢ Recognizing what's important to the search engine
- ➢ How to setup a search engine toolbox that works
- ➢ Understanding how web analytics works
- ➢ How to use Google Analytics the right way

This chapter will help you to understand what Search Engine Optimization (SEO) is all about. You will learn how it will improve your website traffic and grow your business. The first thing you need to know is the SEO process takes time, and you will need to have some patience while you diligently work your SEO strategies daily. Every time you go to the internet to browse for a particular website, the sites that usually come up to the top of your search generally have an SEO strategy working towards that companies' own benefit.

# Let's look at the top 11 search engines in the world at this time

1. **Google-** Google Search Engine is the best search engine globally, and it's also one of the most popular products from Google. Google has acquired almost 70 percent of the Search Engine market.

2. **Bing-** Bing is Microsoft's answer to Google, and it was launched in 2009. Bing is also a good search engine. Bing is the default search engine in Microsoft's web browser.

3. **Yahoo-** Both Yahoo & Bing are not giving competition to Google but giving each other competition. According to the latest report on net market share, Yahoo has a market share of 7.68 percent. Yahoo is still a leader among the most popular free email providers.

4. **Baidu-** Baidu is a Chinese web search engine founded on January 1, 2000. This web search engine is made to deliver results for websites, audio files, and images. Also, Baidu has an Alexa Rank of 4. It also provides some other services, including maps, news, cloud storage, and much more. It is also one of the most used search engines in China.

5. **AOL-** Aol.com is also among the top search engines in the world. It has a market share of 0.59 percent. Verizon Communication has bought AOL for $4.4 billion. It was started back in 1983 as a Control Video Corporation. It was named America Online in 1991 and 2009 as AOL Inc.

6. **Ask.com-** Ask.com was previously known as Ask Jeeves. Its search results are based on question answering web format. It was founded in 1995. It is a question & answer community. Here you can get the answers to your question, and it integrates a large amount of archived data to answer your question.

7. **Excite-** Most of us don't know about a search engine named "Excite." Excite is an online service portal. It provides internet services like email, search engine, news, instant messaging, and weather updates.

8. **DuckDuckGo.com-** DuckDuckGo.com is a popular search engine known for protecting the privacy of users. To generate search results, they have partnered with Yahoo, Bing, and Yummly. It was founded back in 2008 by Gabriel Weinberg.

9. **WolframAlpha.com-** WolframAlpha.com is a computational search engine that does not list documents or web pages as search results. But its results are based on facts & data about that query. It's also called a computational knowledge engine. It was launched in 2009 and is based on Mathematics.

10. **Yandex.com-** Yandex.com is the most used search engine in Russia. It is a Russian internet company. It was launched in 1997. Yandex.com also has a great presence in Ukraine, Kazakhstan, Belarus, and Turkey. It also provides services like Yandex Maps, Yandex Music, online translator, Yandex Money, and many other services.

11. **Lycos.com-** Lycos.com has a good reputation in the search engine industry. It is also a popular search engine founded back in 1995. Its key areas served are email, web hosting, social networking, and entertainment websites.

At this time, these are the best and most popular web search engines in the world. Among them, Google, Bing, and Yahoo dominate the search engine market and have been used by most people in the world. These three are the best search engines to use.

## Search engine terms and details you should understand

- **Relevance-** What this term means is a marketing technique of creating and distributing relevant and valuable content to attract and engage a clearly defined and understood target audience.
- **Spiders or Bots-** The software that search engines use to crawl your site.
- **Crawl-** What a search engine does when it reads and indexes a website.

The search engine wants to deliver the most useful websites relating to the words or information you have put in to search for. This is good for the search engine company and makes the searches relevant to the user. If you want to rank high with the search engine, then make it easy for the search engine to find your site. Let's now look at this information in much more detail.

## Learning what helps a website get a high rank

All search engines look at key phrases and well-written content to determine which websites offer users the best value when they are doing their searches. Well-written content is very important in Google's eyes, as are a decent number of images and strong internal links. If you're consistently publishing good content, steadily acquiring back links, and adding rich media, including images and video, you're taking all the right steps to maintain a solid ranking.

The search engine **spiders or bots** determine the relevance of web pages based on key phrases and some complex rules setup by the search engine company.

When you go to a search engine and type a key phrase like **"Super Cars,"** the search engine will pick the best matches by assessing a few things.

- **The main focus of the website**
- **Site authority on a specific subject**
- **Quality of content writing for the site**
- **Visitor response to the site**

Depending on the key phrase you are searching for, millions of businesses aim to be at the top of the searches by the search engines. But, if you want to fight with the other companies to be at the top, there are some things you must understand about web pages, how they are built, and how search engines read these sites so they get ranked. You want to design your business website in a way that makes it easy for the search engine to find you. And you want to make the website content well written and structured right, so the search engine completely understands what your page and website are all about.

## Some very Important SEO factors

- **Title Tags-** These are at the top of each webpage. They are the first thing search engines look at on your site.
- **Headings-** Headings provide a content outline to the search engines when the bots crawl your pages.
- **Site age-** Remember, older reputable sites generally have a higher ranking. Older sites have more clout than a newer site does.
- **Image captions-** Text captions under or near your images help with searches being done on your site.
- **Links-** When you have links on your site, make sure they are relevant. This makes a huge difference for your business.
- **Social Media-** The importance of social media sites connected to your web pages is super important to your success.
- **Content Quality-** You absolutely must have amazing and quality writing content for all of your web pages to be successful.
- **Website submission-** Submitting your website directly to search engines is a plus, but everything in this section will get you a higher ranking if followed carefully.

**Some important site factors:**

- **Sitemap.** A sitemap helps a search engine to index all pages on your site. It is the simplest and most efficient way to tell Google what pages your website includes.
- **Mobile optimized site.** Only a few years ago, 66% of searchers used mobile exclusively to research interesting sites. This number has increased in the last 12 months. Having a mobile-optimized site can affect rankings in many ways.
- **Google search console integration.** Having your site verified by Google Webmasters Tools is said to help with the indexing of your site. The tool provides valuable data you can use to optimize your site better.

Remember, the SEO process takes time, so you need to make sure the quality of your written content, site links, and social media are perfect. That way, your site will begin to go up in the ranking process over some time.

You absolutely must have amazing and relevant material to gain traction in the ranking process. So, spend plenty of time writing and testing your ideas to see which ones will get you moving in the upward direction in the ranking process.

# Website Tools and Toolkits that enhance the SEO process

**At the top of the list:**
Check out Google Webmaster Tools https://
search.google.com/search-console/about

Here are some of the things you can do once you add your website property:

- Analyze clicks from Google search. Learn more.
- Get alerts for critical errors or issues. Learn more.
- Test whether Google can successfully understand your content.

Microsoft has an amazing free product you may want to try to enhance your SEO Efforts.

## Microsoft Free SEO Toolkit

Start with the free download, review your website, and make changes fast. The SEO Toolkit, with its detailed analysis and search engine friendly suggestions, helps improve the relevance of your website in search results right away.

https://www.microsoft.com/en-us/download/details.aspx?id=24823

## SEO Quake

A powerful SEO Toolbox for your Browser. Check any webpage for a huge selection of SEO parameters with The Free SEO quake. https://www.seo-quake.com/index.html

## Bing Webmaster Tools

Finally, let's look at what Bing has to offer, do more with your site Bing Webmaster provides easy-to-use public tools to help you do more with your site. https://www.bing.com/webmasters/about

As you can see, many of the major search engines have great SEO tools that you can use. These tools use the data search engines collect when they crawl your website to generate detailed reports that can help you with problems your site may be facing and so much more. Take the time to learn all you can about these tools and use them to benefit your business on the web.

## Selecting the right keywords for your web business

In this section, you will learn how to pick the right keywords for your website to bring visitors to your business. To start with, when you're choosing keywords, you need to select them in the mindset of your potential customers and the products or services they will be looking for on your website. You will need to understand what your customers or visitors used to find your product or services. If a customer searches for gaming consoles and clicks a link to your site, they will expect to see something regarding gaming consoles.

Many companies try to optimize their web pages for search by assigning keywords to those pages. The Suggestion for a business picking the right keywords is huge. Keyword selection is fundamental to your success in executing normal searches, paid searches, or Pay per Click PPC campaigns.

Let's now look at five things to think about when choosing your keywords for your website.

- **Focus on good phrases-** Keyword generation should start simply by answering the question of **"What products or services do you sell?"**
- **Avoiding "self-serving" Keywords-** More specific and supportive keywords are going to have a significantly higher conversion rate to purchases on your site.
- **Using Google's Contextual Targeting Tool -** The Contextual Targeting Tool can be accessed by searching and then selecting "Contextual Targeting Tool" under the filter options on the left-hand navigation. What you are presented with now is a visual representation of the way that Google groups together keywords.
- **The importance of repetition-** The more important concept to keep in mind is that you want to choose keywords that best relate to the content present on a web page and a website.
- **Driving your content strategy-** Our keyword research reflects both what users are seeking and how the search engine "thinks" about keywords, we let that help drive our content strategy.

## Understanding and using keyword services and tools

Many search engine optimization companies out there target the right traffic and deliver them to your website. These services have a cost, but they are well worth it if you have the budget to use them. Let's look at some now.

**Google Ad words-** Being seen by customers when they are searching on Google for the things you offer is exactly what Google Ad words do. You only pay when they click to visit your website or make the call. Your business can be found by people on Google exactly when searching for the things you offer.

Site: - https://ads.google.com/home/#!/

**Internet Marketing Ninjas-** We partner with brands to grow visibility, website traffic, and higher search engine rankings through our mixed internet marketing services. No longer "just" the world's greatest link-building company, Internet Marketing Ninjas offers fully-integrated SEO and Internet marketing solutions to meet the demands of the modern digital economy and to take your growth to new heights.

Site: - https://www.internetmarketingninjas.com

Here is a list of 7 free keyword tool service companies you can use to grow and establish your business keyword searches and more.

- https://www.semrush.com
- https://www.spyfu.com
- https://www.wordstream.com
- https://www.wordtracker.com
- https://keywordtool.io
- https://www.link-assistant.com
- https://search.google.com/search-console/about

**Using Google insights-** You've got a vast amount of data at your fingertips. But, do you know what it's telling you? See how to turn data into credible and actionable insights with helpful tools and solutions from Google.

Site: -https://www.thinkwithgoogle.com

## Watching your competition

In this internet business, you always want to watch what the competition is doing. Keep an eye on where your competitors are ranking and monitor the keywords they are using. You should always be looking for ways to take advantage of what the competition is doing and do it even better than they are. If you Google your industry and you will see all of the competition and their rankings.

**Use programs like:**

- https://www.seoquake.com
- https://www.semrush.com
- https://www.spyfu.com

## Keep an eye on your competitors and their methods

If you spend the time enhancing your website better than your competitors, you can rank higher than they can and replace them at the top. Spend some time researching all of the competition to discover if there are ways you can outrank them and be on top. In closing out this section, you should make it your business always to find ways to get to the search engines' top. Not only does this increase your visibility, but you could potentially increase your profits and credibility with your customers and visitors, and this is what truly matters.

## Designing your website for search engines & visitors

This section will help you make your website more appealing to search engines and visitors' buying your products or services. Make sure you are following the basic rules of search engine optimization. Make changes to the page and resubmit it to the search engines when you must. You can submit your pages a maximum of two times per month until you are listed in the major search engine results.

## Powerful content

The best way to get people to link to your site is to provide useful content. First, you need to optimize your code to make it easy for the search engine to see what your page is all about. Next, you need content that makes your site worth linking to, and finally, Get people linking to you right away.

## Content Clustering

Content clustering is a grouping of related content to make your website more relevant to search engines. When you link several related pages together from which your visitors can find those pages on your website, you are creating a cluster. Clustering web pages gives relevance and authority to your website. Remember, the more related pages you link in a cluster, the more authority your website will gain.

What do your visitors want to see? Visitors of your site enjoy finding related content grouped together because it makes the information and search process so much easier.

**Let's now look at the steps actually to create your ranked cluster of web pages.**

1. First, search for all of your web pages that have related content.
2. Make sure you have a single core page that references all of these related pages.
3. You will want to link your core page to the other related pages.
4. Now, you want to link the core page to the home page on your website.

You don't necessarily need to change your entire website. You need to link the related web pages from your site to make it easier for visitors and customers to find what they are looking for on your website. The search engines will be able to see all of the related content, which will make your website more authoritative and relevant.

## Importance of the webpage structure and web links

Once you have completed the proper clustering of your web pages and have your site optimized to SEO marketing standards, you will want to keep and sustain them. You will also want to be aware and make sure that all content and pages for your site are not moved around because this can affect your SEO placement.

Understanding the importance of the **Web Link**. When you write your web links, you should be very specific. The web link tells the visitor what they will see or what information they are going to get when they click or follow the link. When you create your links, make sure they are pointing to the exact content or information the link was designed to address. This is very important to your visitors and for search engines.

We click on a link because we want to complete a task. It's thinking about the customers' journey as they seek to complete a task. It's about making that journey as simple and as fast as possible.

## Why are website URLs very important?

A website URL or domain name is one of the most important parts of your website. If not for this simple string or words that usually end with a .com, .net, or .org, you wouldn't be able to get traffic to your website.

A domain name is the address of your website. This is the one that your visitors are entering on their browsers to get to your site and view your content. Your website's domain name points to your server, which has your website data to access your content. So, without it, your visitors won't be able to locate your website and wouldn't be able to read your content or buy your products or subscribe to your newsletter.

In closing, we have covered a ton of information regarding search engine optimization (SEO) and web analytics. This information is super important for the success of your online business. Try to implement it into your business operations so the stages of the SEO process work for you as you see fit. If things get overwhelming, then hire a professional to assist you in your businesses' success.

# CHAPTER 32

# E-COMMERCE THE FUTURE OF ONLINE SHOPPING & HOW TO GET STARTED TODAY

E-commerce and online shopping are the way of the future for everyone making purchases in America and worldwide. This is important to understand when your customers need to purchase personal items and consumer goods that they use daily. Companies like www.amazon.com, www.walmart.com, www.macys.com, and www.target.com have all jumped from just being just brick and mortar stores to online E-commerce super-stores. Today, E-commerce stores make it very easy and convenient for their customers to purchase their goods and services (24) hours a day from their smart phones, tablets, and laptops. All brick & mortar stores and most shopping malls will have to eventually get online in the E-commerce cloud universe to grow and expand their businesses into the future. Online stores are where everyone that's shopping is purchasing their goods and services and, in particular, the millennial generation who has grown up with computers, technology, and shopping online.

If you want to make money online, you must start an internet business or an E-commerce store that sells amazing products and services that your customers, clients, and social media audience will love and appreciate. We have listed below the top (5) E-commerce steps for your success that you need to understand to succeed when moving your business online and into the cloud.

1.  **Business Logistics-** Business logistics includes creating a cool and catchy name for your business that will be memorable to your customers and that will stand out amongst the crowd. Your logistics process will also include: creating a domain name, an E-commerce website, and setting up specific shopping cart software that works with your E-commerce business so you can accept credit cards and PayPal transactions. There are many different business service providers and shopping cart software vendors to choose from that will cost you less than $500 per year to maintain and operate your business online so you can move forward with your online business ideas. We have searched out some of the best vendors and online host providers listed below for you to review and evaluate.

    - www.amazon.com
    - www.godaddy.com
    - www.shopify.com
    - www.wix.com
    - www.yokart.com
    - www.bigcommerce.com
    - www.woocommerce.com
    - www.tictail.com

    There are many other vendors and business platforms available for you to use that will help you operate your E-commerce store and online business. This is a small list of the most popular vendors on the market that you can consider in your research that could be a good fit for your business needs.

2.  **Finding products to sell-** There are (3) core ways to find products and services to sell on your E-commerce store. Let's take a look at them now.

- **Make and sell the products that you produce-** In this business model, you produce your own products and services for your customers, which you make from your own home or garage. You will produce and sell your products and services directly to your customers from your online store. By operating your business this way, you make 100% pure profit from what you produce and sell to your customers.

- **Buy products or services from a wholesaler-** In this business model, you buy products or services you want to sell from a wholesale manufacturer and then sell them at a higher retail price to your customer base and clients. Check out www.crov.com for more details about your sourcing needs.

- **Drop shipping-** In this business model, you team up with a manufacturing partner who will create products for your customer's On-demand. How it works is when your customers order the products from your site, you will then send these orders to the drop shipping company, and they will drop ship the orders directly to your customer's doorstep. The drop shipping company gets paid by taking a percentage of the sales price on each On-demand order that is made.

This is a great business model because now there is no need for a warehouse to hold your own product inventory. Below is a list of drop shipping companies you can use.

- www.aliexpress.com
- www.salehoo.com
- www.doba.com
- www.wholesale2b.com
- www.worldwidebrands.com
- www.wholesalecentral.com
- www.dropshipper.com
- www.megagoods.com
- www.inventorysource.com

3. **Driving traffic to your site-** Once you have your online store setup with your products and services ready to go, you now will need to drive traffic to your site so you can make money and get paid. You want to use social media to inform the entire world about your business brand and the amazing products and services you're offering to your customers. The proper way to build a following with social media is by consistently creating and producing quality content that invokes your audience and customer base's interest. Once you have your audience's attention, you can now drive them to your E-commerce store and convince them to buy from you. You absolutely need to create amazing content on social media that people will like and want to share with their family and friends.

4. **Brand building-** It's important to build an amazing brand that people will cherish and love. Once you have created your brand, you can then take that product or service to your audience and customers to experience the difference your product brand will make in their lives. Let the value and the benefits of your brand do the selling for you. No one wants to be sold to; people need to believe they are making wise and intelligent purchasing decisions when they're buying products and services they use every day. You want to let your brand be your customer's wise and intelligent decision. That way, they will continue doing business with you regularly.

5. **Setup an affiliate program-** If you want to make huge profits and big sales quickly, you need to get other salespeople to market and promote your branded products and services through an affiliate marketing company. You can have professional salespeople promote your business products and services while making small commissions for every unit they sell to their customers through their affiliate marketing efforts. If you're interested in this business model, you can find out much more information from the affiliate marketing sites below.

- www.clickbank.com
- www.shareasale.com
- www.markethealth.com
- www.jvzoo.com
- https://www.cj.com
- https://affiliate-program.amazon.com

In closing, if you're interested in setting up an E-commerce site or any other type of online business, you need to learn all that you can about business in general and especially about the process of becoming successful in running an E-commerce store. There are many different sites, books, and gurus who can teach you all you need to know about setting up, marketing, and maintaining your online or E-commerce business. All it takes is a little bit of research, careful planning, and a personal commitment to your ideas if you plan on truly succeeding.

# CHAPTER 33

# HOW TO GET CUSTOMERS TO KEEP BUYING FROM YOU

E very business that exists today survives because of its number one asset, its customer base. Without a loyal customer buying your company goods and services, there is no business at all. Smart businesses understand the value of their customers and clients. They try very hard to create and modify their products and services to fulfill their valuable customers' needs.

## The customer is king

If you have a new business and you're just starting out, you must understand the importance of your customers and clients and the value they bring into your business. They are the lifeblood of your business, and they are the very important individuals who are spending their hard-earned money on whatever it is that you're selling to them. You cannot make money without your customers, and you don't have a sustainable business model without them.

## How well do you know your customers?

- What is it that makes your customers happy?
- What pain points do your customers have in their daily lives, and what products or services do you offer to help them solve it?
- How can your products and services add value into the lives of your customers?
- Are your products and services valued at a price that they can afford to pay?

**The steps you can take to keep your business relevant in the market today.**

Do you want to remain relevant in the current marketplace and beat the competition? To sell more goods and services to your customers than your competitors do, you must focus on the five steps to make you more successful than the competition.

1. **Competitive pricing-** People are always looking for the best deals they can find and purchase regarding the pricing of products and services. No one wants to pay more for something that they can find better prices for or at bargain pricing. You must offer your product and services at a better price than your competitors if your business is to remain relevant in the market place. If your competition has better pricing than your business, your customers will go to them instead of you. You can control the market share in your favor when you have excellent prices, and everyone knows it. Try to keep your price as low as possible and make them comparable to your competition so you can maintain your competitive edge.

2. **Great selections and many different options-** People love having various options and buying from companies that have a large selection of choices. One great way to increase your customer base is by

having multiple selections for them to choose from. You want to have a high-quality line of products and services that you offer them and also an economical variety of the same item that you can offer to your customers as well. Having a variety of choices is good for business; it keeps your customers engaged in the shopping experience. You don't want them to become bored while shopping at your store, so make sure your selections appeal to their needs.

3. **High-quality products and services-** Everyone looks for and desires quality when they purchase goods and services. The higher the quality of the products and services, the higher the price you can ask your customers to pay.

**Quality and price go together.** No one wants to spend their hard-earned money on cheap goods and services that they cannot use for an extended period of time. Think about people who shop at Macy's over those who shop at Wal-Mart. When you shop at Macy's, you expect to find higher quality merchandise on hand over what you would expect when shopping at Wal-Mart or Target. Most people go to Wal-Mart or Target because of their discount pricing and the average quality for the items that they carry. Another comparison is the Nike Brand of shoes over other brands of shoes on the market. Nike is known for using high-quality leather in the manufacturing of its shoes that has been tested by athletes all around the world. Their products last a very long time, and that's the reason why people will pay the higher price for the Nike brand over what the competition will charge for the same type of shoes.

4. **The importance of convenience-** People today love convenience when they shop at online stores for the products and services that they're looking for. Just like when shopping online at www.amazon. com, they make it very easy to find what you want, and their prices are super affordable. If your customers have challenges ordering

products and services from your online business and it's not con-venient for them, you will not be in business for much longer. The customer loves convenience. Let's look at some online companies that are doing it right.

- www.amazon.com - Online shopping center
- www.uber.com -Taxi services
- www.grubhub.com - Food delivery services
- www.turo.com – Car rental services

All of these companies offer their customers convenience with the services that they offer their customer base. People love con-venience because of the time and the effort it saves them when they don't have to go out of their way to get what they want. The services offered must be delivered to them with ease of action. If you're in business already or getting ready for startup soon, try to find new ways to make your products and services more convenient for your customers to utilize and get access to. They will appreciate you for it.

5. **Individualized and personalized services-** People love products and services that are individualized and personalized, especially for them, just like when you celebrate your birthday and the birthday cake has your name on it. People feel special on their birthday because things are specifically created for you and only you. Also, think about when you purchase a piece of jewelry with your name or birthstone engraved into it. These items become much more special to you or to the person they were created for because they are per-sonalized for that individual. Another example would be when you go on a cruise ship for a vacation. They are generally personalizing every experience while you're onboard the vessel during the cruise. You are made to feel special and important at the time of your cruise vacation.

In closing, these are the top 5 reasons why customers will continue buying from your business. You must hit a home run with at least the top 3 on this list alone. If you can hit it with all five ideas then, you are guaranteed to be successful with a competitive edge over the competition for a long time to come.

# CHAPTER 34

# THE ABSOLUTE BEST WAYS TO MAKE MONEY ONLINE IN 2020 AND BEYOND

I f you have an idea that you completely believe in and think that you can make money online with this idea, this is the number one business for you. You must make sure that you absolutely believe in your business ideas and your vision. You must plan out every detail of your business strategy through a complete business plan. Since there are so many different ways to make money online, the questions you need to ask yourself are the following.

- **Are you only trying to make money online by any means necessary with no real organic ideas?**
- **Are you trying to start an online business to build up personal wealth for yourself and your family within a special niche' market?**
- **Are you trying to create a business that will make an impact on someone's life by adding value and quality services to them of some kind?**
- **Is this business a type of hobby that you have always wanted to try out?**

You must determine your purpose for starting your online business, and this important information should be detailed within your complete business plan.

Whatever type of business you decide you want to create, you want to try and set it up to produce multiple streams of income for you that will allow you to branch out and cover many different areas of the business world online. This is the ultimate goal of any business to create a means of developing multiple streams of income that pays residuals every month.

## The hottest businesses that are happening right now online

**Affiliate Marketing-** This type of business allows you to promote other people's products or services where you can earn great commissions on each sale by doing so with the ads and the traffic you drive to the product or services. Quality traffic is what you want by creating amazing content and by adding value for those excited customers which may be interested in that product or service. The process of affiliate marketing can take some time to build, so you must be very patient with it to get the desired results. Review some of the best affiliate marketing platforms below. There are many others to choose from so research is the key.

- www.clickbank.com
- https://affiliate-program.amazon.com
- https://www.jvzoo.com

Many other affiliate programs exist today; you need to find the one that excites you the most and the various products or services that you believe in and get started right away.

**Creating Ad marketing-** https://www.google.com/adsense/start In creative Ad marketing, the advertisers are constantly bidding for ad space with millions of other advertisers who compete for ad space. This means that more money, more relevant ads, and more ad spaces get filled regularly. When a You Tuber has a massive audience or a massive following, people will click on the relevant ads on their channel, and you make money from the various Ads. Getting endorsed by a well-known company can generate amazing ad revenue once you have proven yourself in the social media space.

**The rise of E-commerce-** Selling your products online with vendors like Shopify or Amazon is great because the entire world is shopping and buying everything online. No one really goes to the brick and mortar stores as much anymore because shopping online is so much easier. The E-commerce space is the place you want to be if you want to make sales online today.

- https://www.shopify.com
- https://sellercentral.amazon.com

**Drop shipping-** Basically, with drop shipping you will be working with a wholesaler and having them ship products directly to your customers from their warehouse. You drive the traffic to the products or services, and the distributor will ship direct for you to your customers. It's that simple.

- https://www.oberlo.com
- https://alidropship.com

**The software development business-** The software development business is a big business online, and if you have a great idea for something hot or something new that has not be seen before. All you have to do is consult with a software developer and present your ideas to them and bring your software product to life.

- www.fiverr.com
- www.upwork.com
- www.toptal.com

**Skills marketing expert-** In this business model, you provide your customers with knowledge and information that you're very familiar with or have a level of expertise at and package up these skills through webinars, training boot camps, and online classes, etc....

- https://www.gotomeeting.com
- https://clickmeeting.com
- https://www.techsmith.com/store/camtasia

**Video marketing-** This model uses social media platforms such as YouTube and Vimeo to educate, train and teach people about various products and services. You can also earn additional cash flow by using Google Ad-sense on your channel to get small amounts of money from Ad promotions. Marketing the right products or services on YouTube can generate huge profits for those who have a large following. Personal branding is a huge moneymaker by creating videos for company products and doing consumer evaluations. Many You Tuber's make a killing this way. Creating brand awareness is loved by many YouTube viewers.

- www.youtube.com
- https://vimeo.com
- https://www.dailymotion.com/us

In closing, there are many different ways to make money online, as you can see. Take some time to research the one opportunity that works best for you, and once you have the knowledge, skills, and education you need. You can plan out your vision and make it happen on the various social media platforms that's the best fit for you and your business model.

# CHAPTER 35

# DIGITAL MARKETING
## THE HOTTEST BUSINESS IN THE 21ST CENTURY

The digital marketing field is super-hot right now! It's one of the best fields to be in right now for anyone or any age group, and you can make great money with it as well. The 2 questions to think about are.

- What does it take to be a digital marketing expert today?
- What does it take to make money at it and become successful?

## Learning how to use social media to grow your business and sell your products or services

- You need to start with and discover what your niche' market will be for your business model. In other words, you will need to discover who your customers are? And what is it that you would like to sell to them? You also need to discover what known social media platforms do your customers and clients communicate on? You must also know who will want to buy the products or services you're bringing to the market. You need to research and discover if you should be selling your products or services on <u>YouTube?</u> Should you be selling your products and services to the crowd on Facebook? Or, is <u>Twitter</u> where your customers communicate and share their thoughts and ideas? If you're selling a peer-to-peer product or service, then is <u>LinkedIn</u> where you should be looking to setup and start communicating.

- <u>www.youtube.com</u>
- <u>www.facebook.com</u>
- <u>https://twitter.com</u>
- <u>https://www.linkedin.com</u>

- The second thing you must do is build up a following with your customer base and clients by offering something valuable to them. For you do this successfully, you must join the proper social media platform where your audience comes together regularly and communicate with them. You need to regularly communicate with them to get the necessary feedback on their personal interests, pain points, and what their passions are. You must discover what your customers, your followers, and your clients enjoy doing in their spare time? You must discover what issues or pain points do they have right now going on in their lives? Once you have a clear understanding about all of this very important information, you will now be able to tailor your product ideas and your services towards a solution for your customer base within your niche' market.

- You must make valuable and exciting offers to your audience with your products and services to meet their needs and bring about solutions to their pain points. It's very important to make your audience feel much better about themselves or help them to feel better about their lives in some very important way. If you manage this process properly with a great amount of care and bring about satisfaction and joy to your audience, this is where you can close the sale, which is exactly what you wanted all along. You must offer them something to buy from you that can solve a problem and bring about satisfaction into their lives. People will spend whatever amount of money possible to solve a problem or solve a pain point within their lives.

## Understanding how business people use social media

Most business people use social media mainly to make money and grow their businesses. The average person will use it to build up a following for themselves or just to make some new friends. Which reason are you going to use social media for in your future? The same way that the business person does, which is to make money? Or are you going to use it to gain some followers and make some new friends?

If you're in business for yourself, it should be obvious that social media should be used as a tool to build up a following towards gaining support for your products and services within your niche market. You must use wisdom and a strategic marketing strategy to make money with your followers when you use these various platforms. These social media platforms can also enhance your personal life with the right following that appreciates your products, services, and personal brand. In the process of developing and building up a following for your business, the offers you present to your audience can help you keep your wealth moving in an upward direction, if done properly.

# An age-old marketing trick
# that keeps on working

### How to use scarcity and limited timed offers to sell to customers

Using scarcity and limited timed offers is an advanced and psychological way of selling to your customers and getting them to act in a specific way. Most people don't want to feel like they are missing out on an opportunity of getting something special that they think is needed. Psychologists have long known that you can make consumer goods more desirable by making them appear to be a rare commodity. When you're using this scarcity method to sell to your customers, they need to believe that they should act right away; otherwise, they may miss out on the opportunity of a lifetime. You are attempting to control the supply and the demand to get individuals to take action as you need them to.

The greatest salespeople in the world and many of the very large corporations that exist today use this technique all the time, and they make a killing doing it as well.

Try to use the scarcity concept or limited timed offers with your products and services and see how it works out for you.

Human behavior is such that we are likelier to purchase something if we're informed that it's the very last one or that a special deal will soon expire. The point is that if people believe that they will be missing out on something, they will be prompted to act more quickly to receive it.

**Some cool scarcity ideas from www.Booking.com. Here are a few scarcity ads at play here**

- **"Lock in this great price while you still can"** – Implies this deal won't be around for long.
- **"Booked 26 times today"** – Tells you this hotel is desirable.
- **"5 people are looking right now"** – Tells you there may be some competition for the offer.
- **"You missed it!"** – Oh, Wow, this one is already gone. I better beat out the others for the next offer I see.
- **"In high demand – only four rooms left on our site!"** – This is the most obvious scarcity example I could show you.

In closing, learn as much as you can about the digital marketing field, and once you have it mastered, you can then apply the best techniques available.

You will be able to see your finances and wealth potential shoot through the roof practically overnight once everything is setup and operational.

For some very low and discount training in the field of digital marketing, please take a look at some of the resources we have provided you with below.

- Udemy- https://www.udemy.com/courses/marketing/digital-marketing
- For some great digital marketing books and resources to look at, go to- www.amazon.com

# THE HOTTEST CAREER CHOICES THAT WILL HAVE A FUTURE IN THE 21ST CENTURY & BEYOND

Since the corona virus epidemic began in November of 2019, it has now changed every Americans way of life in less than 12 months. This is a huge change for most Americans and also for billions of people all over the world. Because of these rapid changes, there are some career decisions we will all have to evaluate to discover if these careers will still be relevant in the future once this epidemic has subsided.

By the year 2030, many of the automation systems and robotic technologies that are on the rise and that exist even today will be in full operation and used by many companies and various industries worldwide. There is a massive ramp-up currently to get these automation systems installed and in place to replace human resources within the next five to ten years. Many of the different reports that you can read online for yourself have detailed that there will be massive layoffs coming soon. There will be a removal of more than 20 million jobs by the time these robotic technologies and the automation systems are fully up and operational.

Let's now take a look at some career choices that will definitely be impacted by these automation and robotic system changes that you need to be aware of.

- Travel agents
- Cashiers
- Fast-food workers
- Mail services
- Production and factory workers
- Retailers
- Dispatchers operators
- Lumberjacks
- Telemarketers
- Legal secretaries
- Fishermen

This information should be important to everyone because these changes can affect our livelihood going forward, and you want to be prepared for the future. We need to all realize that technology is on the rise, and it's also here to stay; these technologies are moving at a very rapid pace. We need to understand these changes very carefully because we could get left behind if we don't. You don't want your career or family to be an afterthought because you didn't change with the times and understand what was going on when it was happening.

## What does the future look like? - Understanding the past and the future of global workers.

Here are some facts for you to think about to begin preparing your mind for the future.

| The Past | The Future |
| --- | --- |
| Working a 9-5 job | Open working hours |
| Working in a corporate office | Working from home or remotely |
| Following office, politics | Leading your own operations |
| Managers and supervisors | You are the manager of your own projects |
| Corporate training sessions | Learning on your own with online training |

## Workers of the future

**Freelance and contract workers-** By the year 2027 and beyond, freelance workers and contract workers will have a majority of the existing available jobs. This is the skills-based economy where a person works for themselves within the hours they choose rather than working directly through a company with office hours and office politics. Within this type of position, you must develop an online portfolio of your working abilities and skills. Companies need to know if you're capable and if you can deliver as promised. Sometimes you must work for free just to market yourself in this line of freelance and contract work. If you're highly skilled and need to get your name out into the market, we have listed below some of the best platforms to establish yourself.

- **www.fiverr.com**
- **www.upwork.com**
- **www.toptal.com**
- **www.freelancer.com**
- **www.skyword.com**
- **www.peopleperhour.com**

**Affiliate Marketing-** Affiliate marketing allows you to make money while you're sleeping once you setup everything and have it running on autopilot. This is a highly desirable field for many young people and digital marketers alike. Affiliate marketing is a tactic that drives sales to a specific product or service and generates sales commissions for your efforts. You can make small and sometimes even very large commissions for marketing someone else's product or services. You need to search for the product or services you believe in, promote that product or service, and earn profits from each sale.

**Some benefits of Affiliate Marketing**

- **Has very low startup cost**
- **You can work from anywhere in the world**

- **No product inventory or customer support needed**
- **Earn excellent commissions for your efforts**

**The best Affiliate Marketing programs**

- **www.clickbank.com**
- **www.cj.com**
- **www.shareasale.com**
- **www.affiliate-program.amazon.com**
- **www.partnernetwork.ebay.com**

**Digital Marketing-** Within the digital marketing field, there are many different ways to make money at it online. Digital marketing is by far one of the hottest fields to learn about and understand that will make you a ton of money if you learn how to do it correctly.

**Some digital marketing career choices to choose from**

- **Search engine optimization (SEO)**
- **Content creation**
- **Digital Advertising**
- **Retargeting and marketing**
- **Social media marketing**
- **Email marketing**
- **Affiliate marketing**
- **Web analytics**

These are just a few of the different areas within the digital marketing field that you can make money if you know what you're doing. You will need to learn and understand which segment appeals to you the most? You will then have to dive in headfirst to gain the proper skills to be successful at your craft. The digital marketing field is huge and growing larger and larger every year because of the type of money that can be made. Discover for yourself if the digital marketing field is right for you. If you need to gain the necessary skills to be successful, here are some online training and learning centers that can get you there.

- www.udemy.com
- www.udacity.com
- www.edx.org
- www.coursera.org
- www.skillshare.com

In closing, the world is changing very quickly. Those individuals who are highly skilled and very aware of these changes will be at the top of their game. And for those people who don't care to know about these changes or those individuals who are asleep right now in their lives. This technology may just pass them by and make them irrelevant or an afterthought in the future. You must keep your knowledge and skills up to date and be aware of what's coming if you want to remain relevant and keep money flowing in your direction.

# CHAPTER 37

# UNDERSTANDING THE INDUSTRIES THAT WILL CONTINUE TO GROW
## PAST THE CORONA VIRUS PANDEMIC

W orld Trade Organization (WTO) - Predicted that global trade will decrease by 13% or more by the end of 2020. They foresee this pandemic as having some extensive negative effects on the world economies for some time to come.

It is a known fact that the rich are getting richer for those who are paying very close attention and those who understand that there will be many wealthy people who will come out of this **Corona Virus Pandemic** even wealthier than they were before the pandemic even started. What do they know, and what are they doing that's so different than the rest of the people within our society? How can they have an edge over the rest of us and take advantage of the opportunities within this terrible time?

## Things are changing very quickly

Because of the challenges of this pandemic, things are changing very quickly. For many of the corporate workers, regular employees, and college students that are living across this country and the world at large, are starting to work more remotely because of the nature of this pandemic and the social distancing requirements, and the many other issues that (COVID 19) has presented. To curb the effects and the impact of this virus, working remotely is the best viable option right now. This shift will have a global impact on many businesses heavily dependent on their workers to commute to their jobs every day. One of the issues that many corporations have noticed is that since so many people work remotely, no one is consuming as many of the items they used to while commuting. This shift is now having a global impact on the worldwide economy.

This global pandemic will reshape many businesses for decades to come. Let's now look at some of the businesses that will survive and thrive after this pandemic is over and long gone. These are some of the fields that the rich and the wealthy may be involved in or financing to stay ahead of the curve.

- **The digital marketing field-** This very popular field has downsized a little because of this pandemic's chaotic effects. Since the world operates on and from computers and many businesses are operating online, digital marketing is set to thrive post (COVID 19). If you want to remain relevant and succeed in the future, digital marketing is one of the best ways to do that. You should learn as much as you can about the different facets of this business model and upgrade your skill-set coming out of this pandemic to make the kind of money that you would like for your future.

- **E-commerce businesses-** E-commerce is where everyone is doing their shopping in today's marketplace. The brick and mortar stores have suffered greatly since this pandemic started, and they weren't doing so great for the past few years. There are many reports of popular brick and mortar stores and restaurants that closed their doors permanently because of this outbreak. Most of the stores that have an online presence will weather the storm created by this pandemic. Try to think of an idea that will work for you and create an online business that will generate some profit and try to get it up and running a quickly as possible. You want to prepare yourself for the coming financial struggles that so many people will have to face.

- **Freelance workers-** Freelance workers, are working in what is known as the gig economy, where they operate within some short-term contracts instead of working on set hours or permanent jobs. Instead of getting a regular salary, these workers are paid by the project or by the gig that they can get done and completed. You must be highly skilled within the gig economy if you're going to be able to compete and make money at it.

- **Stock market investors-** At this time, money and lending may be tightly affected by this pandemic, but coming out of it, you may want to learn how to grow your wealth by learning all that you can about stocks, bonds, mutual funds, ETF's and Bitcoin. The very wealthy individuals within our society have always had their feet planted heavily within the stock market, and so should you.

- **Online learning and education-** This pandemic has affected many businesses and college universities alike within cities worldwide. Online education and online learning are a far better asset to you and more cost-effective for most people over the cost of going to a brick and mortar college university in another state that had to shut down due to this pandemic. There are many options to choose from. You will just have to discover which one works best for you and your work schedule. Below are some discounts and free options to choose from.

1. www.khanacademy.org
2. www.udemy.com
3. www.coursera.org
4. www.edx.org

5. www.udacity.com
6. www.skillshare.com

- **Food and agriculture fields-** One of the biggest threats caused by the pandemic is the lack of food products that couldn't make it to the stores on time when the pandemic struck. The important need for people to grow their own food and to start their own gardens became a big deal as soon as the Corona Virus lockdown happened. The food disruptions caused prices to skyrocket, and shortages were a major problem as well.

- **Product delivery services-** The delivery business and logistic company services are in high demand right now, with everyone on lockdown and stuck at home. From people who deliver boxes, clothing and food supplies, and every other type of packaging service that's out there right now. There is a ton of money in the delivery business right now if you can find the right niche.

- **Medical solution providers-** The right type of business that will help people overcome and prevent sickness from the Corona Virus is a great business to be in right now. Hand sanitizer manufacturers and mask producers are making a killing right now since the virus started. This is all due to the demand for personal protective equipment (PPE) needs within our society right now.

- **Live and home streaming services-** Businesses like Netflix, Hulu, HBOMax, crackle, and Amazon Prime have been expanding since the virus has kept many people off work and at home. If you have an idea to stream movies, you will make money. This is an expanding and growing field right now.

- **The gaming industry-** Since the pandemic started, gaming platforms like Sony play station and others have increased their traffic exponentially, practically overnight. If you have a gaming idea, now is the time to bring that idea to the market place; there is money to be made.

- **Health and fitness industry-** People who promote fitness and those who create supplements are in high demand right now since the Corona Virus has started. If you have anything that will help boost people's immune systems during this pandemic, you will make money for sure. The health industry is booming right now.

In closing, those who are paying real close attention and those who will take the necessary action based on what's happening right now will make money and become the next millionaires. If you're concerned about the future and about what industries will survive and remain strong after this pandemic is over. We have just listed the 11 industries that for sure will survive and be in demand going into the future. If you can somehow try to get into one of these industries, you may be able to make a ton of money. One thing is for sure that things are never going to be the same again. Many of our known habits will have to change and evolve post-Corona Virus (COVID 19).

# CHAPTER 38

# CAMPAIGNING FOR THE RIGHT OUTREACH CAUSES

For those entrepreneurs that are new to starting their own online businesses and new to the world of digital marketing, one of the best and easiest ways to increase your social media following and increasing your new customer base is by supporting and joining human outreach programs and campaigns that matter most to those within your community and the world in general.

When you align your business and join in the fight against cancer or you're helping to support those organizations that are fighting to keep children safe from homelessness and sexual predators. The world will see your business through a different lens. Those companies that align themselves with the various outreach programs that exist today will begin to be recognized as they partner with and strengthen the organizations for those people that are struggling the most right now in their lives. You will also be viewed as a pillar within the community that you operate from when it comes to the support that you give on behalf of those individuals who are less fortunate within our society.

## What outreach programs should I support and partner with?

Whenever you decide to take this approach with supporting human outreach programs, you should first think about what outreach programs matter the most to you and which ones are doing the work you believe in. We have listed some great causes that are in constant need of support due to the heavy influx of challenges that affect so many people within our society for you to choose from.

- Homeless and hunger outreach programs
- Cancer support outreach programs
- Child abuse and child trafficking outreach programs
- Drug addiction and depression outreach programs
- Domestic violence outreach programs
- Supporting American Veterans outreach programs

There are so many different types of outreach programs within our society and around the world that require financial and volunteering support. You just need to find the one that you believe in and contact them with whatever type of support you would like to give.

## There are four main types of support that you can offer outreach programs that they will appreciate.

- **Volunteering support-** When people don't have much money or physical resources available, volunteering is the perfect type of support which many outreach programs value that they will never turn away from and will always appreciate.
- **Financial support-** Financial support is, by far, one of the best and easiest ways to support any outreach program. With the money, they can pay for whatever resources they need to keep the outreach up and operational.

- **Product support-** If you are a company that manufactures blankets for example, you can donate a percentage of your products to support those organizations that help the homeless and disaster relief organizations that need blankets. This would be a donation and a business write-off for you as well.
- **Services support-** If you happen to have an IT business with a cyber security team, you could offer your services to an outreach program to keep them up and operational whenever they need it. This would help the outreach maintain their business infrastructure with these types of services.

Once you have decided on what type of support you are capable of offering the outreach program, you will want to contact a local branch of that organization and explain the level of support you can offer. You want to explain at what frequency these products or services will be available to them, and once the terms are agreed upon, your partnership can begin.

The television stations and local media corporations love to give coverage and the spotlight to those organizations that support human outreach efforts. You can use this media attention in your favor to enhance your existing marketing efforts and bring a positive light to your business and to those outreach programs that you believe in that are very important to you.

In closing, if you want to expand and grow your business, think deeply about supporting and partnering with local outreach programs or local charities within your community that you believe in. There are many other known benefits to supporting outreach programs other than just positive publicity. You can also gain some amazing tax breaks through a (501) C3 charitable donation slip that can save your business some money at the end of each year. Get started today and support your local outreach programs.

# CHAPTER 39

# HOW TO PROPERLY MANAGE YOUR BUSINESS DURING A CRISIS

As of July 2020, many businesses may now have to scrap their business plans and the business model they started with and restructure it to survive post-Corona Virus (Covid 19), or they will have to close their doors completely if they cannot figure out how to survive after the pandemic has ended.

There are many businesses worldwide now trying to figure out how they can survive and move forward while the world is in shutdown mode. Lockdowns are happening in various cities across the United States and worldwide. Many of the stressed-out business owners are panicking because they don't know what to do or how to move forward right now.

## The two things that all business leaders and innovators need to do with their businesses right now.

Right now is not the time to panic, but it is time to evaluate and take full control over whatever you have left of your business on the table to survive this crisis. Here are some very important steps you can take to come out of this global crisis with your business intact and possibly with your doors still open.

1.  **Monitor and control your spending habits-** Today, you must carefully evaluate what money you still have coming into the business your (revenue), and you must understand what cost and (expenses) you have going out at this time as well, which is critical to your businesses survival. Right now, is the time to conserve and save as much money and capital as you can while things are uncertain. It's not the time to make any major investments until the market corrects itself and stability is back on the rise. You must minimize your risk at this time at all costs.

2.  **Unload assets that are not producing-** When the Corona Virus crisis struck, many businesses had to shut down completely and layoff many, if not all, of their loyal employees. The financial pressure for those businesses that were already struggling before the pandemic may not be able to open back up all of their businesses operations at once. Some companies will have to sell off parts of their business that are not generating revenue, holding the company back from its potential success. It will help if you let go of your business segments that are not profitable right now.

## Start automating business operations going forward into the future.

We live in the digital age of doing business today, where so many businesses and companies operate online and in the cloud. You may need to carefully evaluate your business model to discover what parts of your business operations or what part of your company's products and services can you automate and make it into a digital service or digital package.

## Think about reducing your human dependency to make your business more efficient in a crisis.

This is not an easy thing to think about when it comes to layoffs and downsizing. The idea here is to analyze your business operations to see if there are any ways to reduce your headcount by way of automated systems or robotic technologies. In many cases, the automated systems are just as efficient as a person would be doing the same job or running the same type of machine. You want to try and find a way to make your business more efficient by utilizing systems that can replace bodies that require extensive health costs, retirement payments, and insurance costs. In a crisis, you want to be able to lower your human headcount to protect the cost of running your business and use more automated systems if that's even possible.

## Balancing the company books is critical when your business is in a crisis.

Now that you have taken control over your business and your operational spending, you've sold off assets that are not producing revenue. Once you have automated your business segments that can be automated, it's now time to check your cash reserves and balance your books. You must have cash on hand to survive in a crisis. Your liquid cash flow will help you manage this crisis and get you through your challenges during this pandemic. You must know where your cash is coming from (cash inflow) and where it's going out (expenses). You must discover which vendors you work with that owe you money so you can collect that cash flow as well as everyone else who owes you money through your accounts receivables.

## Try to renegotiate your existing deals with your vendors

In a crisis, everyone is under pressure, and many businesses are struggling, so you want to try and renegotiate some of your existing deals with your vendors to see if they make you a better deal or better offer in this crisis. You can get some pretty good deals when businesses are desperate to increase their cash flow to remain in business. You want to do this for your business because no one knows how long this crisis will last. Negotiate with your vendors to see what can happen. It just may work out in your favor.

## Appreciating your valued and important customers

All businesses that exist does so because of their valuable customer base and their clientele. In a crisis, you must pay homage to your customer base and realize that they may be experiencing some of the same challenges that you're facing within your business. Many of them have been laid off and are now struggling financially. There may be overdue bills, and they may even have late payments on things that they use every day. Try to think about what you can do in their time of need to comfort your customer base. You want to try to be the bridge between their problems and the solution that they are looking for. Try to add value with your existing customers to show them that you care about what happens to them and their families.

In closing, nothing is for certain within a crisis, so you must carefully evaluate your business operations and cut back on things you don't need. Going forward, try to automate your business as much as you can, and you want to still support your valued customers through the end of this crisis. They will appreciate and remember you for it.

# CHAPTER 40

# THE SALES FUNNEL USING IT TO YOUR ADVANTAGE

W hat is a sales funnel, and how do you use it to your advantage for the success of your business? Good question.

A sales funnel is a software program and process that takes a visitor to your online business through a step-by-step sales process.

**The basic components of a sales funnel**

- Opt-in or squeeze page
- A landing page
- A sales page
- Thank you, page,
- Download page
- Order confirmation page

**The opt-in or squeeze page most important components**

- First name
- Last name
- Email address

You can create and set up many different types of sales funnels for your business based on the various business operations or the various products and services you're trying to sell to your customers. The sales funnel process begins with your product or service or both, depending on your business model.

## The basic sales funnel process

### Step 1

**The opt-in page or the squeeze page-** With this type of sales page, you are bringing in traffic to your website from your various solo ads, classic marketing, and social media marketing efforts through this page. The objective is to get the visitor's email so you can send them future offers when you want to. The opt-in or squeeze page is critical to your success because it can make or break your business traffic, especially for those visitors who are new and organic to your business looking for solutions through your products and services.

### Step 2

**The thank-you page is-** Thanking the visitor for Opting in and signing up with their email for your valuable and informative information. It's also showing gratitude for the trust your customers are displaying with you and your business.

### Step 3

**The landing or business page-** After you have snagged the visitor's email and you have thanked them for opting in. Next, you want to send them to your special or amazing offer page or your website where your product or services are so you can now make and close on a sale.

## The automated sale funnels

To be successful with the sale funnel process, you could try to make a run at it alone by learning from scratch, but why? There are some unique systems are already available to help you manage and design your business sales funnel process for you. You could take a look at the best of them below.

- www.clickfunnels.com
- www.getresponse.com
- www.simvoly.com
- www.groovefunnels.com

There are many other automated sales funnel products and sites available for the success of your business. You just need to research and discover which one is right for you and your business model.

## The Auto-Responder

The auto responder is an email program that manages emails for you individually and works in conjunction with the sales funnels process to manage and process emails for very large group emails that need to be sent out to your visitors, customer, or clients. The auto responder will automatically answer emails for you. Let's take a look at some auto responder vendors you can use for your business.

- www.activecampaign.com
- www.getresponse.com
- www.constantcontact.com
- www.aweber.com
- www.mailerlite.com
- www.sendinblue.com
- www.mailchimp.com

In closing, if you want to gain more visitors and automate the sales process, you absolutely need to implement a sales funnel process for your business to succeed in the digital age. All you need to do is learn about the sales funnel process and use the automated systems that already exist within the program, and use them in your favor for your business's success.

# CHAPTER 41

# THE EMPOWERMENT RESOURCES
## FREE & LOW-COST EDUCATIONAL RESOURCES

For each website that we have listed below, some of the training options are for free, while others charge a small fee for their training and business resources. Each institution offers something valuable to you, but one thing for sure; you will gain a wealth of knowledge and information from whatever option you choose to go with.

www.udemy.com - The world's largest selection of free and low-cost courses choose from over 100,000 online video courses with new editions published every month.

www.khanacademy.org - Get a university-level education and training for free; Khan Academy is well known and one of the best around and it is FREE!

www.futurelearn.com -Unlock new opportunities with unlimited access to hundreds of online short courses for a year.

https://www.barclaycollege.edu - Students at this private Christian college in Kansas attend for free if they live on campus. All students – including international students – who live in a dorm qualify for the college's full-tuition scholarship.

www.codecademy.com - The Easiest Way to Learn to Code.

www.open.edu/openlearn - Search for free courses, interactive videos and more.

https://realwaystoearnmoneyonline.com - Discounted work at home training.

www.coursera.org - From Courses to Degrees 100% online learning from the best universities and companies, it's free to join. www.edx.org - Accelerate your future. Learn anytime, anywhere, it's free to join, and they have many free pieces of training and programs.

www.cbtnuggets.com - Learn On-Demand Training for IT Professionals.

www.skillshare.com - Thousands of classes to fuel your creativity and career.

www.udacity.com - industry-leading programs built and recognized by top companies worldwide.

www.cybrary.it - Build your Cyber Security or IT career, For Free.

www.ciebookstore.com - Learn from home Courses, Labs, DVDs, and more.

www.vtc.com - Learn any software with ease.

www.scitraining.com - Stratford Career Institute- The affordable way to Train from Home.

www.impactpublications.com - The One-Stop Career, Life Skills, and More.

www.planetcdrom.com -Quality, full-version discount software at the best possible price. The majority of our products are FREE. No membership clubs to join and no obligation to buy anything else. Just pay for Shipping and Delivery!

www.georgebrown.ca- has many technical and distant learning programs to choose from, such as the following below:

- Their Electronic Technician Training: www.etcourse.com
- Automation Technical Training: www.automationprogram.com
- Electro-Mechanical Technician Training: www.emcourse.com
- Robotics Technical Training: www.onlinerobotics.com
- Programmable Logic Controllers Training: www.plctechnician.com

## Personal Growth & Empowerment Resources

Each resource that we have listed below has something different and equally amazing to read about and offer to you. They will add value into your life and completely change your mental paradigm. You don't have to think exactly like everyone else; you can think for yourself. You will gain a wealth of knowledge and information from each resource.

- **Think Like a Monk- Book by Jay Shetty**
- **The Gift of Forgiveness- Book by Katherine Schwarzenegger**
- **Get Out of Your Head- Book by Jennie Allen**
- **Didn't See That Coming- By Rachel Hollis**
- **Living Your Best Life Now- By Sterlyn Smith**
- **Help Self- By Tanya Hennessy**

## Personal Growth websites to Consider

Zen Habits- https://zenhabits.net If you're looking for ways to calm the chaos surrounding your life, consider Zen Habits. This website contains lifestyle choices that will make you happier and more productive.

Tiny Budda- https://tinybuddha.com Tiny Buddha is full of inspirational content about relationships, happiness, mindfulness, healthy habits, and much more.

Success- https://www.success.com This self-improvement website focuses on becoming successful.

Addicted to Success- https://addicted2success.com Teaches you how to achieve your goals.

The Positivity Blog- https://www.positivityblog.com Turn your life around by focusing on happiness and positivity.

Life Hack- https://www.lifehack.org This site is full of life tips that will make your day easier.

## Business Resources

Business knowledge is at the core of every business and corporation that exists on earth. We have a list of some of the best resources available to help you with your business startup, business support, and business mentorship. Find the one that's right for you in your quest to start your own business.

**www.sba.gov** - Small Business Administration- A government organization dedicated to helping small business owners start and grow their businesses; they offer many information and a ton of resources. The SBA Definitely a great place to start for anyone wanting to start their own business.

**www.score.org** - Business Success Starts Here SCORE is the nation's largest network of volunteer, expert business mentors, with more than 10,000 volunteers in 300 chapters. Get the mentorship you have always wanted and maybe even need.

**www.business.com** - CONNECTING YOU TO OPPORTUNITY. They are an organization ready to empower your business.

**www.legalzoom.com** - Where life meets legal. They can help you with business formation and business setup. They can help you setup your business for a fee, of course.

**www.501c3.org** - We Help Nonprofits Thrive! Non-profit Formations. They can help you with Form 990 and the State Charity Registration. They have Bookkeeping services as well.

**www.onevest.com** - Whether you are an investor seeking to build your portfolio with potentially high-return investment opportunities or an entrepreneur is seeking resources to build your company, and the Onevest Ecosystem can help.

**www.quora.com** -Some of the most reputable entrepreneurs and leaders in the tech industry come here to dole out information, making it among the best websites to get your questions answered.

**https://angel.co** - Angel List - the platform for new companies to get equity from reliable investors; it also features templates to minimize attorney fees.

**www.allbusiness.com** -This site is rich with advice and tips for just about everything an entrepreneur may need to know. They offer many things, from office etiquette to internet marketing.

## Business Software

No business can run itself without its business technology, business software, and business systems. Since every business runs differently, you must evaluate the best options that will help you propel your organization into the future and beyond. Below we have a small list of some of the popular software programs and sites that can help you decide what may be best for your business organization.

https://www.capterra.com - Finding software is complicated. Simplify it with Capterra. From accounting to zookeeping, Capterra is software selection simplified.

https://www.liveplan.com - The world's leading business plan software, built for entrepreneurs like you. Also, https://www.businessplanpro.com

https://quickbooks.intuit.com - Simple accounting software. This software is shockingly easy to use. Many small businesses use this for their bookkeeping and accounting system.

https://www.microsoft.com/en-us - Office 2016 Home & Business 2019 - $249.99

https://turbotax.intuit.com - Turbo Tax, for all of your tax needs.

https://keap.com/infusionsoft - Ranked #1 out of 50 for Small Businesses. Over 200K small business users trust Infusion soft to organize and automate their processes. Put it to work and free up time to grow your business.

www.bamboohr.com -automates operational tasks and frees HR to perform the big-picture projects that make a difference.

www.zoho.com – Zoho gives you one integrated suite of apps for your entire organization. Decide which apps to use based on your requirements. Then deploy them to your employees through our centralized Admin Panel. You can get it all for one simple, affordable price.

https://monday.com - Simplify how your team works and manages your workload, communicate with your team, and celebrate success.

## Business Empowerment books

There are thousands of books on business to choose from on the market. All of them will offer you something different that you may benefit from.

You must do your careful research and choose the best one for you and your business model. A good place to start is with. www.amazon.com

## Credit & Credit Repair Resources

**You need to know and understand the power of your credit and the credit report-** Otherwise known as your financial report card. Credit is very important in life, if you will become a borrower with a bank or financial institution. You need to monitor your credit carefully and never let your debts ever get out of hand if you can prevent it.

**The big three credit bureaus**

- https://www.experian.com
- https://www.equifax.com
- https://www.transunion.com

**The credit repair organizations that can help you**

- https://www.creditkarma.com
- https://www.creditrepair.com
- https://www.lexingtonlaw.com
- https://www.lexingtonlaw.com
- https://skybluecredit.com

## Finance & Investing Sites & Resources

Like the many business books on the market, there are tons of books and websites on all types of finance and investment strategies you can make for yourself. Since we're all not in the same financial situation in our lives right now. Not all of them will work for you or for your own personal financial strategy. We have listed some of the best resources for beginners who would like an easy, simple process to get their finances and investments knowledge and skill developed.

https://www.m1finance.com - Free automated investing. M1 Finance empowers you to manage your money and build wealth with ease.

https://tradegenius.co - Learn to Trade and Make Money Nearly Every Day. The BEST Stock Market & Cryptocurrency Training Programs Online!

https://www.fxcm.com/markets/forex/what-is-forex - Take a closer look at Forex Trading, and you may find some exciting trading opportunities unavailable with other investments.

https://www.babypips.com - The beginner's guide to FX trading, NEWS, TRADING, EDUCATION

https://www.betterment.com - Our mission is to help our customers maximize their money. Whether you're new to investing or a seasoned pro, Betterment does what is right for you and your money. Our retirement recommendations could increase returns by 1.61% compared to those of the typical investor.

https://fundrise.com - Unlock a new world of real estate investing. You can invest your money, according to your goals, in a portfolio filled with dozens of real estate projects — each one carefully handpicked and proactively developed to grow your net worth.

https://www.robinhood.com - Invest Commission-Free Invest in stocks, ETFs, options, and cryptocurrencies, all commission-free, right from your phone or desktop.

https://www.firstrade.com - Brokerage Account. Build your family's wealth with an Individual or Joint brokerage account.

https://www.webull.com - Webull Financial LLC. Invest Smart · Trade Free.

## Finance & Investment books

Upon doing your careful research, whatever financial or investment options, books, or other resources you choose to read, all of them will offer you some specific knowledge, wisdom, and understanding regarding business, finances, and investing. All you need to do is understand the basic concepts and principles within the reading and then apply what you have learned to reap the knowledge and benefits fully. Get started today. A great place to start for doing your research is with www.amazon.com

# The End

Thank you for reading

*Getting Your Business on Track in the Digital Age*

# ABOUT THE AUTHOR

*Sterlyn M. Smith*

Sterlyn Markell Smith is the author behind *"Living Your Best Life Now"* and *"Getting Your Business On Track in The Digital Age."* He is also a father who believes in the good of humanity. Sterlyn has a Degree in Electronic Engineering and is a certified IT Professional and a business owner that has a passion for awakening and empowering people who are getting started with their first online business. Sterlyn Smith is an artist, videographer, photographer, and a writer who currently lives and works in Las Vegas, Nevada. His work across multiple disciplines broadly addresses different narratives around the human experience, which drives his empowerment business success. As an author, Sterlyn hopes to create something that educates, inspires, and motivates his readers. Sterlyn has a ton of passion for seeing people rise to their fullest potential and make a difference in the minds of those individuals who are struggling and hurting the most. Sterlyn's main focus is sharing things that matter and awakening the minds of those who need it in their own lives.

www.ingramcontent.com/pod-product-compliance
Lightning Source LLC
Chambersburg PA
CBHW071337210326
41597CB00015B/1477